ALSO BY LES MURRAY

The Vernacular Republic: Selected Poems
The Daylight Moon and Other Poems
The Rabbiter's Bounty: Collected Poems
The Boys Who Stole the Funeral: A Novel Sequence
Dog Fox Field
Translations from the Natural World
Subhuman Redneck Poems
Fredy Neptune: A Novel in Verse
Learning Human: Selected Poems
Conscious and Verbal
Poems the Size of Photographs
The Biplane Houses
Taller When Prone
Killing the Black Dog

NEW SELECTED POEMS

New Selected Poems

LES MURRAY

Farrar, Straus and Giroux
New York

Farrar, Straus and Giroux
18 West 18th Street, New York 10011

Printed in the United States of America
A shorter version was first published in Australia in 2007 as *Selected Poems* by
Black Inc., Australia
This version was originally published, in slightly different form, in 2012
by Carcanet Press Limited, Great Britain
Published in the United States by Farrar, Straus and Giroux
First American edition, 2014

'The Black Beaches' was first published in *Hermes* (Australia); 'Inspecting the
Rivermouth' in *Quadrant* (Australia) and *First Things* (USA); 'High Rise' in
The Spectator (UK); 'Nuclear Family Bees' in *Chimaera* (Australia); 'When
Two Per Cent Were Students' in *Quadrant* (Australia); 'I Wrote a Little Haiku'
in *The Rialto* (UK); 'West Coast Township' in *The Times Literary Supplement*
(UK); 'Money and the Flying Horses' in *The Spectator* (UK); 'Sun Taiko' in
Australian Poetry Journal; 'Child Logic' in *Qualm* (UK); 'Powder of Light' in
Quadrant (Australia) and *Little Star* (USA).

Library of Congress Cataloging-in-Publication Data
Murray, Les A., 1938–
    [Poems. Selections]
    New selected poems / Les Murray. — First American edition.
        pages   cm
    Includes index.
    ISBN 978-0-374-22088-4 (Hardcover)
    1. Australian poetry—21st century.   I. Title.

PR9619.3.M83A6 2014
821'.912—dc23

                                                2013044344

www.fsgbooks.com
www.twitter.com/fsgbooks • www.facebook.com/fsgbooks

1   3   5   7   9   10   8   6   4   2

to the glory of God

Contents

NEW SELECTED POEMS

The Burning Truck

i.m. Mrs Margaret Welton

It began at dawn with fighter planes:
they came in off the sea and didn't rise,
they leaped the sandbar one and one and one
coming so fast the crockery they shook down
off my kitchen shelves was spinning in the air
when they were gone.

They came in off the sea and drew a wave
of lagging cannon-shells across our roofs.
Windows spat glass, a truck took sudden fire,
out leaped the driver, but the truck ran on,
growing enormous, shambling by our street-doors,
coming and coming . . .

By every right in town, by every average
we knew of in the world, it had to stop,
fetch up against a building, fall to rubble
from pure force of burning, for its whole
body and substance were consumed with heat
but it would not stop.

And all of us who knew our place and prayers
clutched our verandah-rails and window-sills,
begging that truck between our teeth to halt,
keep going, vanish, strike . . . but set us free.
And then we saw the wild boys of the street
go running after it.

And as they followed, cheering, on it crept,
windshield melting now, canopy-frame a cage
torn by gorillas of flame, and it kept on
over the tramlines, past the church, on past
the last lit windows, and then out of the world
with its disciples.

Driving Through Sawmill Towns

1

In the high cool country,
having come from the clouds,
down a tilting road
into a distant valley,
you drive without haste. Your windscreen parts the forest,
swaying and glancing, and jammed midday brilliance
crouches in clearings . . .
then you come across them,
the sawmill towns, bare hamlets built of boards
with perhaps a store,
perhaps a bridge beyond
and a little sidelong creek alive with pebbles.

2

The mills are roofed with iron, have no walls:
you look straight in as you pass, see lithe men working,

the swerve of a winch,
dim dazzling blades advancing
through a trolley-borne trunk
till it sags apart
in a manifold sprawl of weatherboards and battens.

The men watch you pass:
when you stop your car and ask them for directions,
tall youths look away –
it is the older men who
come out in blue singlets and talk softly to you.

Beside each mill, smoke trickles out of mounds
of ash and sawdust.

3

You glide on through town,
your mudguards damp with cloud.
The houses there wear verandahs out of shyness,
all day in calendared kitchens, women listen
for cars on the road,
lost children in the bush,
a cry from the mill, a footstep –
nothing happens.

The half-heard radio sings
its song of sidewalks.

Sometimes a woman, sweeping her front step,
or a plain young wife at a tankstand fetching water
in a metal bucket will turn round and gaze
at the mountains in wonderment,
looking for a city.

4

Evenings are very quiet. All around
the forest is there.
As night comes down, the houses watch each other:
a light going out in a window here has meaning.

You speed away through the upland,
glare through towns
and are gone in the forest, glowing on far hills.

On summer nights
ground-crickets sing and pause.
In the dark of winter, tin roofs sough with rain,
downpipes chafe in the wind, agog with water.
Men sit after tea
by the stove while their wives talk, rolling a dead match
between their fingers,
thinking of the future.

An Absolutely Ordinary Rainbow

The word goes round Repins,
the murmur goes round Lorenzinis,
at Tattersalls, men look up from sheets of numbers,
the Stock Exchange scribblers forget the chalk in their hands
and men with bread in their pockets leave the Greek Club:
There's a fellow crying in Martin Place. They can't stop him.

The traffic in George Street is banked up for half a mile
and drained of motion. The crowds are edgy with talk
and more crowds come hurrying. Many run in the back streets
which minutes ago were busy main streets, pointing:
There's a fellow weeping down there. No one can stop him.

The man we surround, the man no one approaches
simply weeps, and does not cover it, weeps
not like a child, not like the wind, like a man
and does not declaim it, nor beat his breast, nor even
sob very loudly — yet the dignity of his weeping

holds us back from his space, the hollow he makes about him
in the midday light, in his pentagram of sorrow,
and uniforms back in the crowd who tried to seize him
stare out at him, and feel, with amazement, their minds
longing for tears as children for a rainbow.

Some will say, in the years to come, a halo
or force stood around him. There is no such thing.
Some will say they were shocked and would have stopped him
but they will not have been there. The fiercest manhood,
the toughest reserve, the slickest wit amongst us

trembles with silence, and burns with unexpected
judgements of peace. Some in the concourse scream
who thought themselves happy. Only the smallest children
and such as look out of Paradise come near him
and sit at his feet, with dogs and dusty pigeons.

Ridiculous, says a man near me, and stops
his mouth with his hands, as if it uttered vomit –
and I see a woman, shining, stretch her hand
and shake as she receives the gift of weeping;
as many as follow her also receive it

and many weep for sheer acceptance, and more
refuse to weep for fear of all acceptance,
but the weeping man, like the earth, requires nothing,
the man who weeps ignores us, and cries out
of his writhen face and ordinary body

not words, but grief, not messages, but sorrow,
hard as the earth, sheer, present as the sea –
and when he stops, he simply walks between us
mopping his face with the dignity of one
man who has wept, and now has finished weeping.

Evading believers, he hurries off down Pitt Street.

Working Men

Seeing the telegram go limp
and their foreman's face go grey and stark,
the fettlers, in their singlets, led him
out, and were gentle in the dark.

Vindaloo in Merthyr Tydfil

The first night of my second voyage to Wales,
tired as rag from ascending the left cheek of Earth,
I nevertheless went to Merthyr in good company
and warm in neckclothing and speech in the Butcher's Arms
till Time struck us pintless, and Eddie Rees steamed in brick lanes
and under the dark of the White Tip we repaired shouting

to I think the Bengal. I called for curry, the hottest,
vain of my nation, proud of my hard mouth from childhood,
the kindly brown waiter wringing the hands of dissuasion
O vindaloo, sir! You sure you want vindaloo, sir?
But I cried Yes please, being too far in to go back,
the bright bells of Rhymney moreover sang in my brains.

Fair play, it was frightful. I spooned the chicken of Hell
in a sauce of rich yellow brimstone. The valley boys with me
tasting it, croaked to white Jesus. And only pride drove me,
forkful by forkful, observed by hot mangosteen eyes,
by all the carnivorous castes and gurus from Cardiff
my brilliant tears washing the unbelief of the Welsh.

Oh it was a ride on Watneys plunging red barrel
through all the burning ghats of most carnal ambition
and never again will I want such illumination
for three days on end concerning my own mortal coil

but I signed my plate in the end with a licked knife and fork
and green-and-gold spotted, I sang for my pains like the free
before I passed out among all the stars of Cilfynydd.

Incorrigible Grace

Saint Vincent de Paul, old friend,
my sometime tailor,
I daresay by now you are feeding
the rich in Heaven.

The Pure Food Act

Night, as I go into the place of cattle.

Night over the dairy
the strainers sleeping in their fractions,
vats
and the mixing plunger, that dwarf ski-stock, hung.

On the creekstone cement
water driven hard through the Pure Food Act
dries slowest round tree-segment stools,
each buffed
to a still bum-shine,
sides calcified with froth.

Country disc-jocks
have the idea. Their listeners aren't all human.
Cows like, or let their milk for, a firm beat
nothing too plangent (diesel bass is good).

Sinatra, though, could calm a yardful of horns
and the Water Music
has never yet corrupted honest milkers
in their pure food act.

The quiet dismissal switching it off, though,
and carrying the last bucket, saline-sickly
still undrinkable raw milk to pour in high
for its herringbone and cooling pipe-grid
fall
to the muscle-building cans.

His wedding, or a war,
might excuse a man from milking
but milk-steeped hands are good for a violin
and a cow in rain time is
a stout wall of tears.

But I'm britching back.

I let myself out through the bail gate.
Night, as I say.
Night, as I go out to the place of cattle.

József

M.J.K. 1882–1974 In Piam Memoriam

You ride on the world-horse once
no matter how brave your seat
or polished your boots, it may gallop you
into undreamed-of fields

but this field's outlandish: Australia!
To end in this burnt-smelling, blue-hearted
metropolis of sore feet and trains
(though the laughing bird's a good fellow).

Outlandish not to have died
in king-and-kaiserly service,
dismounted, beneath the smashed guns
or later, with barons and credit

after cognac, a clean pistol death.
Alas, a small target, this heart.
Both holes were in front, though, entry
and exit. I learned to relish that.

Strange not to have died with the Kingdom
when Horthy's fleet sank, and the betting
grew feverish, on black and on red,
to have outlived even my Friday club

and our joke: *senilis senili*
gaudet. I bring home coffee now.
Dear God, not one café in this place,
no Andrássy-street, no Margaret's Island . . .

no law worth the name: they are British
and hangmen and precedent–quibblers
make rough jurisprudence at best.
Fairness, of course; that was their word.

I don't think Nature speaks English.
I used to believe I knew enough
with *gentleman*, *whisky*, *handicap*
and perhaps *tweed*. French lacked all those.

I learned the fine detail at seventy
out here. Ghosts in many casinos
must have smiled as I hawked playing cards
to shady clubs up long stairways

and was naturalized by a Lord Mayor
and many bookmakers, becoming a
New Australian. My son claims he always
was one. We had baptized him Gino

in Hungary. His children are natives
remote as next century. My eyes
are losing all faces, all letters,
the colours go, red, white, now green

into Hungary, Hungary of the poplar trees
and the wide summers where I am young
in uniform, riding with Nelly,
the horseshoes' noise cupping our speeches.

I, Mórelli József Károly,
once attorney, twice gunshot, thrice rich,
my cigarettes, monogrammed, from Kyriazi,
once married (dear girl!) to a Jew

(gaining little from that but good memories
though my son's uniforms fitted her son
until it was next year in Cape Town)
am no longer easy to soften.

I will eat stuffed peppers and birds' milk,
avoid nuns, who are monstrous bad luck,
write letters from memory, smoke Winstons
and flex my right elbow at death

and, more gently, at living.

Kiss of the Whip

In Cardiff, off Saint Mary's Street,
there in the porn shops you could get
a magazine called Kiss of the Whip.
I used to pretend I'd had poems in it.

Kiss of the Whip. I never saw it.
I might have encountered familiar skills
having been raised in a stockwhip culture.
Grandfather could dock a black snake's head,

Stanley would crack the snake for preference
leap from his horse grab whirl and jolt!
the popped head hummed from his one-shot slingshot.
The whips themselves were black, fine-braided,

arm-coiling beasts that could suddenly flourish
and cut a cannibal strip from a bull
(millisecond returns) or idly behead an
ant on the track. My father did that.

A knot in the lash would kill a rabbit.
There were decencies: good dogs and children
were flogged with the same lash doubled back.
A horsehair plait on the tip for a cracker

sharpened the note. For ten or twelve thousand
years this was the sonic barrier's
one human fracture. Whip-cracking is that:
thonged lightning making the leanest thunder.

When black snakes go to Hell they are
affixed by their fangs to carved whip-handles
and fed on nothing but noonday heat,
sweat and flowing rumps and language.

They writhe up dust-storms for revenge
and send them roaring where creature comfort's
got with a touch of the lash. And that
is a temple yard that will bear more cleansing

before, through droughts and barracks, those
lax, quiet-speaking, sudden fellows
emerge where skill unbraids from death
and mastering, in Saint Mary's Street.

The Broad Bean Sermon

Beanstalks, in any breeze, are a slack church parade
without belief, saying *trespass against us* in unison,
recruits in mint Air Force dacron, with unbuttoned leaves.

Upright with water like men, square in stem-section
they grow to great lengths, drink rain, keel over all ways,
kink down and grow up afresh, with proffered new greenstuff.

Above the cat-and-mouse floor of a thin bean forest
snails hang rapt in their food, ants hurry through several dimensions:
spiders tense and sag like little black flags in their cordage.

Going out to pick beans with the sun high as fencetops, you find
plenty, and fetch them. An hour or a cloud later
you find shirtfulls more. At every hour of daylight

appear more that you missed: ripe, knobbly ones, fleshy-sided,
thin-straight, thin-crescent, frown-shaped, bird-shouldered,
    boat-keeled ones,
beans knuckled and single-bulged, minute green dolphins at suck,

beans upright like lecturing, outstretched like blessing fingers
in the incident light, and more still, oblique to your notice
that the noon glare or cloud-light or afternoon slants will uncover

till you ask yourself Could I have overlooked so many, or
do they form in an hour? unfolding into reality
like templates for subtly broad grins, like unique caught expressions,

like edible meanings, each sealed around with a string
and affixed to its moment, an unceasing colloquial assembly,
the portly, the stiff, and those lolling in pointed green slippers . . .

Wondering who'll take the spare bagfulls, you grin with happiness
– it is your health – you vow to pick them all
even the last few, weeks off yet, misshapen as toes.

The Mitchells

I am seeing this: two men are sitting on a pole
they have dug a hole for and will, after dinner, raise
I think for wires. Water boils in a prune tin.
Bees hum their shift in unthinning mists of white

bursaria blossom, under the noon of wattles.
The men eat big meat sandwiches out of a styrofoam
box with a handle. One is overheard saying:
drought that year. Yes. Like trying to farm the road.

The first man, if asked, would say *I'm one of the Mitchells.*
The other would gaze for a while, dried leaves in his palm,
and looking up, with pain and subtle amusement,

say *I'm one of the Mitchells.* Of the pair, one has been rich
but never stopped wearing his oil-stained felt hat. Nearly everything
they say is ritual. Sometimes the scene is an avenue.

The Powerline Incarnation

When I ran to snatch the wires off our roof
hands bloomed teeth shouted I was almost seized
held back from this life
                  O flumes   O chariot reins
you cover me with lurids deck me with gaudies feed
my coronal   a scream sings in the air
above our dance   you slam it to me with farms
that you dark on and off numb hideous strong friend
Tooma and Geehi freak and burr through me
rocks fire-trails damwalls mountain-ash trees slew
to darkness through me   I zap them underfoot
with the swords of my shoes
                        I am receiving mountains
piloting around me   Crackenback   Anembo
the Fiery Walls   I make a hit in towns
I've never visited: smoke curls lightbulbs pop grey
discs hitch and slow   I plough the face of Mozart
and Johnny Cash   I bury and smooth their song
I crack it for copper links and fusebox spiders
I call my Friend from the circuitry of mixers
whipping cream for a birthday I distract the immortal
Inhuman from hospitals
                to sustain my jazz
and here is Rigel in a glove of flesh
my starry hand discloses smoke, cold Angel.
Vehicles that run on death come howling into
our street with lights a thousandth of my blue
arms keep my wife from my beauty   from my species
the jewels in my tips
              I would accept her in
blind white remarriage cover her with wealth
to arrest the heart   we'd share Apache leaps
crying out *Disyzygy!*
             shield her from me, humans
from this happiness I burn to share   this touch
sheet car   live ladder   wildfire garden shrub –
away off I hear the bombshell breakers thrown

diminishing me   a meaninglessness coming
over the circuits
                    the god's deserting me
but I have dived in the mainstream   jumped the graphs
I have transited the dreams of crew-cut boys named Buzz
and the hardening music
                        to the big bare place
where the strapped-down seekers, staining white clothes, come
to be shown the Zeitgeist
                        passion and death my skin
my heart all logic   I am starring there
and must soon flame out
                        having seen the present god
It who feels nothing   It who answers prayers.

Creeper Habit

On Bennelong Point
a two-dimensional tree
drapes the rock cutting.

Bird-flecked, self-espaliered
it issues out of the kerb
feeding on dead sparks
of the old tram depot;

a fig, its muscles
of stiffened chewing gum grip
the flutings and beads
of the crowbar-and-dynamite wall.

The tree has height and extent
but no roundness. Cramponned in cracks
its branches twine and utter
coated leaves.

With half its sky blank rock
it has little choice.
It has climbed high from a tiny sour gall
and spreads where it can,
feeding its leaves on the light
of North Shore windows.

Employment for the Castes in Abeyance

I was a translator at the Institute:
fair pay, clean work, and a bowerbird's delight
of theory and fact to keep the forebrain supple.

I was Western Europe. *Beiträge, reviste,
dissertaties, rapports* turned English under my
one-fingered touch. Teacup-and-Remington days.

It was a job like Australia: peace and cover,
a recourse for exiles, poets, decent spies,
for plotters who meant to rise from the dead with their circle.

I was getting over a patch of free-form living:
flat food round the midriff, long food up your sleeves –
castes in abeyance, we exchanged these stories.

My Chekhovian colleague who worked as if under surveillance
would tell me tales of real life in Peking and Shanghai
and swear at the genders subsumed in an equation.

The trade was uneasy about computers, back then:
if they could be taught not to render, say, *out of sight
out of mind* as *invisible lunatic*

they might supersede us – not
because they'd be better. More on principle.
Not that our researchers were unkindly folk:

one man on exchange from Akademgorod
told me about Earth's crustal plates, their ponderous
inevitable motion, collisions that raised mountain chains,

the continents rode on these Marxian turtles, it seemed;
another had brought slow death to a billion rabbits,
a third team had bottled the essence of rain on dry ground.

They were translators, too, our scientists:
they were translating the universe into science,
believing that otherwise it had no meaning.

Leaving there, I kept my Larousse and my Leutseligkeit
and I heard that machine translation never happened:
language defeated it. We are a language species.

I gather this provoked a shift in science,
that having become a side, it then changed sides
and having collapsed, continued at full tempo.

Prince Obolensky succeeded me for a time
but he soon returned to Fiji to teach Hebrew.
In the midst of life, we are in employment:

seek, travel and print, seek-left-right-travel-and-bang
as the Chinese typewriter went which I saw working
when I was a translator in the Institute.

Driving to the Adelaide Festival 1976
via the Murray Valley Highway

A long narrow woodland with channels, reentrants, ponds:
the Murray's a mainstream with footnotes, a folklorists' river.

The culture, on both banks, is pure Victoria:
the beer, the footy, the slight earnest flavour, the cray.

Some places there's a man–made conventional width of water
studded with trunks; a cold day in the parrots' high rooms.

Walking on the wharf at Echuca, that skyscraper roof:
sixty feet down timber to a dry-season splash.

In the forest there are sudden cliffs: dusty silken water
moving away: the live flow is particle-green.

Billabongs are pregnant with swirls, and a sunken road
of hyacinth leads to an eerie noonday corner.

Ships rotting in the woods, ships turning to silt in blind channels;
one looked like a bush pub impelled by a combine header.

Out in the wide country, channels look higher than the road
even as you glance along them. Salt glittering out there.

Romance is a vine that survives in the ruins of skill:
inside the horizon again, a restored steamboat, puffing.

Thinking, at speed among lakes, of a time beyond denim
and the gardens of that time. Night-gardens. Fire gardens.

Crazed wood, brushed chars, powder-blue leaves. Each year the
    purist
would ignite afresh with a beerbottle lens, a tossed bumper –

Heading for a tent show, thinking stadium thoughts,
a dense bouquet slowing the van through the province of sultanas.

The Buladelah-Taree Holiday Song Cycle

1

The people are eating dinner in that country north of Legge's Lake;
behind flywire and venetians, in the dimmed cool, town people
  eat Lunch.
Plying knives and forks with a peek-in sound, with a tuck-in
  sound,
they are thinking about relatives and inventory, they are talking
  about customers and visitors.
In the country of memorial iron, on the creek-facing hills there,
they are thinking about bean plants, and rings of tank water, of
  growing a pumpkin by Christmas;
rolling a cigarette, they say thoughtfully Yes, and their
  companion nods, considering.
Fresh sheets have been spread and tucked tight, childhood rooms
  have been seen to,

for this is the season when children return with their children
to the place of Bingham's Ghost, of the Old Timber Wharf, of
  the Big Flood That Time,
the country of the rationalized farms, of the day-and-night farms,
  and of the Pitt Street farms,
of the Shire Engineer and many other rumours, of the tractor
  crankcase furred with chaff,
the places of sitting down near ferns, the snake-fear places, the
  cattle-crossing-long-ago places.

2

It is the season of the Long Narrow City; it has crossed the
  Myall, it has entered the North Coast,
that big stunning snake; it is looped through the hills, burning all
  night there.
Hitching and flying on the downgrades, processionally balancing
  on the climbs,

it echoes in O'Sullivan's Gap, in the tight coats of the flooded-
  gum trees;
the tops of palms exclaim at it unmoved, there near Wootton.

Glowing all night behind the hills, with a northshifting glare,
    burning behind the hills;
through Coolongolook, through Wang Wauk, across the
    Wallamba,
the booming tarred pipe of the holiday slows and spurts again;
    Nabiac chokes in glassy wind,
the forests on Kiwarrak dwindle in cheap light; Tuncurry and
    Forster swell like cooking oil.
The waiting is buffed, in timber villages off the highway, the
    waiting is buffeted:
the fumes of fun hanging above ferns; crime flashes in strange
    windscreens, in the time of the Holiday.
Parasites weave quickly through the long gut that paddocks shine
    into;
powerful makes surging and pouncing: the police, collecting
    Revenue.
The heavy gut winds over the Manning, filling northward,
    digesting the towns, feeding the towns;
they all become the narrow city, they join it;
girls walking close to murder discard, with excitement, their names.
Crossing Australia of the sports, the narrow city, bringing home
    the children.

3

It is good to come out after driving and walk on bare grass;
walking out, looking all around, relearning that country.
Looking out for snakes, and looking out for rabbits as well;
going into the shade of myrtles to try their cupped climate,
swinging by one hand around them,
in that country of the Holiday . . .

stepping behind trees to the dam, as if you had a gun,
to that place of the Wood Duck,
to that place of the Wood Duck's Nest,
proving you can still do it; looking at the duck who hasn't seen
    you,
the mother duck who'd run Catch Me (broken wing)
I'm Fatter (broken wing), having hissed to her children.

The birds saw us wandering along.

Rosellas swept up crying out *we think we think*; they settled
farther along;

knapping seeds off the grass, under dead trees where

their eggs were, walking around on their fingers, flying on into
the grass.

The heron lifted up his head and elbows; the magpie stepped
aside a bit,

angling his chopsticks into pasture, turning things over in his head.

At the place of the Plough Handles, of the Apple Trees Bending
Over, and of the Cattlecamp,

there the vealers are feeding; they are loosely at work, facing
everywhere.

They are always out there, and the forest is always on the hills;

around the sun are turning the wedgetail eagle and her mate, that
dour brushhook-faced family:

they settled on Deer's Hill away back when the sky was opened,

in the bull-oak trees way up there, the place of fur tufted in the
grass, the place of bone-turds.

5

The Fathers and the Great-grandfathers, they are out in the
paddocks all the time, they live out there,

at the place of the Rail Fence, of the Furrows Under Grass, at
the place of the Slab Chimney.

We tell them that clearing is complete, an outdated attitude, all
over;

we preach without a sacrifice, and are ignored; flowering bushes
grow dull to our eyes.

We begin to go up on the ridge, talking together, looking at the
kino-coloured ants,

at the yard-wide sore of their nest, that kibbled peak, and the
workers heaving vast stalks up there,

the brisk compact workers; jointed soldiers pour out then, tense
with acid; several probe the mouth of a lost gin bottle;

Innuendo, we exclaim, *literal minds!* and go on up the ridge,
announced by finches;

passing the place of the Dingo Trap, and that farm hand it
    caught, and the place of the Cowbails,
we come to the road and watch heifers,
little unjoined Devons, their teats hidden in fur, and the cousin
    with his loose-slung stockwhip driving them.
We talk with him about rivers and the lakes; his polished horse is
    stepping nervously,
printing neat omegas in the gravel, flexing its skin to shake off flies;
his big sidestepping horse that has kept its stones; it recedes
    gradually, bearing him;
we murmur *stone-horse* and *devilry* to the grinners under grass.

6

Barbecue smoke is rising at Legge's Camp; it is steaming into the
    midday air,
all around the lake shore, at the Broadwater, it is going up
    among the paperbark trees,
a heat-shimmer of sauces, rising from tripods and flat steel, at that
    place of the cone shells,
at that place of the Seagrass, and the tiny segmented things
    swarming in it, and of the Pelican.
Dogs are running around disjointedly; water escapes from their
    mouths,

confused emotions from their eyes; humans snarl at them
    Gwanout and Hereboy, not varying their tone much;
the impoverished dog people, suddenly sitting down to nuzzle
    themselves; toddlers side with them:
toddlers, running away purposefully at random, among cars, into
    big drownie water (come back, Cheryl-Ann!).
They rise up as charioteers, leaning back on the tow-bar; all their
    attributes bulge at once:
swapping swash shoulder-wings for the white-sheeted shoes that
    bear them,
they are skidding over the flat glitter, stiff with grace, for once
    not travelling to arrive.
From the high dunes over there, the rough blue distance, at
    length they come back behind the boats,
and behind the boats' noise, cartwheeling, or sitting down, into
    the lake's warm chair;

they wade ashore and eat with the families, putting off that
    uprightness, that assertion,
eating with the families who love equipment, and the freedom
    from equipment,
with the fathers who love driving, and lighting a fire between
    stones.

7

Shapes of children were moving in the standing corn, in the
    child-labour districts;
coloured flashes of children, between the green and parching
    stalks, appearing and disappearing.
Some places, they are working, racking off each cob like a lever,
    tossing it on the heaps;
other places, they are children of child-age, there playing jungle:
in the tiger-striped shade, they are firing hoehandle machine-
    guns, taking cover behind fat pumpkins;
in other cases, it is Sunday and they are lovers.
They rise and walk together in the sibilance, finding single rows
    irksome, hating speech now,

or, full of speech, they swap files and follow defiles, disappearing
    and appearing;
near the rain-grey barns, and the children building cattleyards
    beside them;
the standing corn, gnawed by pouched and rodent mice;
    generations are moving among it,
the parrot-hacked, medicine-tasselled corn, ascending all the
    creek flats, the wire-fenced alluvials,
going up in patches through the hills, towards the Steep Country.

8

Forests and State Forests, all down off the steeper country;
    mosquitoes are always living in there:
they float about like dust motes and sink down, at the places of
    the Stinging Tree,
and of the Staghorn Fern; the males feed on plant-stem fluid,
    absorbing that watery ichor;
the females meter the air, feeling for the warm-blooded smell,
    needing blood for their eggs.

They find the dingo in his sleeping-place, they find his
    underbelly and his anus;
they find the possum's face, they drift up the ponderous pleats of
    the fig tree, way up into its rigging,
the high camp of the fruit bats; they feed on the membranes and
    ears of bats; tired wings cuff air at them;
their eggs burning inside them, they alight on the muzzles of cattle,
the half-wild bush cattle, there at the place of the Sleeper Dump,
    at the place of the Tallowwoods.
The males move about among growth tips; ingesting solutions,
    they crouch intently;
the females sing, needing blood to breed their young; their
    singing is in the scrub country;
their tune comes to the name-bearing humans, who dance to it
    and irritably grin at it.

9

The warriors are cutting timber with brash chainsaws; they are
    trimming hardwood pit-props and loading them;
Is that an order? they hoot at the peremptory lorry driver, who
    laughs; he is also a warrior.
They are driving long-nosed tractors, slashing pasture in the
    dinnertime sun;
they are fitting tappets and valves, the warriors, or giving finish to
    a surfboard.
Addressed on the beach by a pale man, they watch waves break
    and are reserved, refusing pleasantry;
they joke only with fellow warriors, chaffing about try-ons and
    the police, not slighting women.
Making Timber a word of power, Con-rod a word of power,
    Sense a word of power, the Regs. a word of power,
they know belt-fed from spring-fed; they speak of being *stiff*, and
    being *history*;
the warriors who have killed, and the warriors who eschewed
    killing,
the solemn, the drily spoken, the life peerage of endurance;
    drinking water from a tap,
they watch boys who think hard work a test, and boys who think
    it is not a test.

10

Now the ibis are flying in, hovering down on the wetlands,
on those swampy paddocks around Darawank, curving down in
    ragged dozens,
on the riverside flats along the Wang Wauk, on the Boolambayte
    pasture flats,
and away towards the sea, on the sand moors, at the place of the
    Jabiru Crane;
leaning out of their wings, they step down; they take out their
    implement at once,
out of its straw wrapping, and start work; they dab grasshopper
    and ground-cricket
with nonexistence . . . spiking the ground and puncturing it . . .
    they swallow down the outcry of a frog;
they discover titbits kept for them under cowmanure lids, small
    slow things.
Pronging the earth, they make little socket noises, their
    thoughtfulness jolting down and up suddenly;
there at Bunyah, along Firefly Creek, and up through Germany,
the ibis are all at work again, thin-necked ageing men towards
    evening; they are solemnly all back
at Minimbah, and on the Manning, in the rye-and-clover
    irrigation fields;
city storemen and accounts clerks point them out to their wives,
remembering things about themselves, and about the ibis.

11

Abandoned fruit trees, moss-tufted, spotted with dim lichen
    paints; the fruit trees of the Grandmothers,
they stand along the creekbanks, in the old home paddocks,
    where the houses were,
they are reached through bramble-grown front gates, they creak
    at dawn behind burnt skillions,
at Belbora, at Bucca Wauka, away in at Burrell Creek, at
    Telararee of the gold-sluices.
The trees are split and rotten-elbowed; they bear the old-
    fashioned summer fruits,
the annual bygones: china pear, quince, persimmon;
the fruit has the taste of former lives, of sawdust and parlour
    song, the tang of Manners;

children bite it, recklessly,
at what will become for them the place of the Slab Wall, and of
the Coal Oil Lamp,
the place of moss-grit and swallows' nests, the place of the
Crockery.

12

Now the sun is an applegreen blindness through the swells, a
white blast on the sea face, flaking and shoaling;
now it is burning off the mist; it is emptying the density of trees,
it is spreading upriver,
hovering about the casuarina needles, there at Old Bar and
Manning Point;
flooding the island farms, it abolishes the milkers' munching breath
as they walk towards the cowyards; it stings a bucket here, a
teatcup there.
Morning steps into the world by ever more southerly gates;
shadows weaken their north skew
on Middle Brother, on Cape Hawke, on the dune scrub toward
Seal Rocks;
steadily the heat is coming on, the butter-water time, the
clothes-sticking time;
grass covers itself with straw; abandoned things are thronged with
spirits;
everywhere wood is still with strain; birds hiding down the creek
galleries, and in the cockspur canes;
the cicada is hanging up her sheets; she takes wing off her
music-sheets.
Cars pass with a rational zoom, panning quickly towards
Wingham,
through the thronged and glittering, the shale-topped ridges, and
the cattlecamps,
towards Wingham for the cricket, the ball knocked hard in front
of smoked-glass ranges, and for the drinking.
In the time of heat, the time of flies around the mouth, the time
of the west verandah;
looking at that umbrage along the ranges, on the New England
side;
clouds begin assembling vaguely, a hot soiled heaviness on the
sky, away there towards Gloucester;

a swelling up of clouds, growing there above Mount George, and
above Tipperary;

far away and hot with light; sometimes a storm takes root there,
and fills the heavens rapidly;
darkening, boiling up and swaying on its stalks, pulling this way
and that, blowing round by Krambach;
coming white on Bulby, it drenches down on the paddocks, and
on the wire fences;
the paddocks are full of ghosts, and people in cornbag hoods
approaching;
lights are lit in the house; the storm veers mightily on its stem,
above the roof; the hills uphold it;
the stony hills guide its dissolution; gullies opening and
crumbling down, wrenching tussocks and rolling them;
the storm carries a greenish-grey bag; perhaps it will find hail and
send it down, starring cars, flattening tomatoes,
in the time of the Washaways, of the dead trunks braiding water,
and of the Hailstone Yarns.

13

The stars of the holiday step out all over the sky.
People look up at them, out of their caravan doors and their
campsites;
people look up from the farms, before going back; they gaze at
their year's worth of stars.
The Cross hangs head-downward, out there over Markwell;
it turns upon the Still Place, the pivot of the Seasons, with one
shoulder rising:
'Now I'm beginning to rise, with my Pointers and my Load . . .'
hanging eastwards, it shines on the sawmills and the lakes, on the
glasses of the Old People.
Looking at the Cross, the galaxy is over our left shoulder, slung
up highest in the east;
there the Dog is following the Hunter; the Dog Star pulsing
there above Forster; it shines down on the Bikies,

and on the boat-hire sheds, there at the place of the Oyster; the
place of the Shark's Eggs and her Hide;
the Pleiades are pinned up high on the darkness, away back
above the Manning;
they are shining on the Two Blackbutt Trees, on the rotted river
wharves, and on the towns;
standing there, above the water and the lucerne flats, at the place
of the Families;
their light sprinkles down on Taree of the Lebanese shops, it
mingles with the streetlights and their glare.
People recover the starlight, hitching north,
travelling north beyond the seasons, into that country of the
Communes, and of the Banana:
the Flying Horse, the Rescued Girl, and the Bull, burning
steadily above that country.
Now the New Moon is low down in the west, that remote
direction of the Cattlemen,
and of the Saleyards, the place of steep clouds, and of the Rodeo;
the New Moon who has poured out her rain, the moon of the
Planting-times.
People go outside and look at the stars, and at the melon-rind
moon,
the Scorpion going down into the mountains, over there towards
Waukivory, sinking into the tree-line,
in the time of the Rockmelons, and of the Holiday . . .
the Cross is rising on his elbow, above the glow of the horizon;
carrying a small star in his pocket, he reclines there brilliantly,
above the Alum Mountain, and the lakes threaded on the Myall
River, and above the Holiday.

The Gum Forest

After the last gapped wire on a post,
homecoming for me, to enter the gum forest.

This old slow battlefield: parings of armour,
cracked collars, elbows, scattered on the ground.

New trees step out of old: lemon and ochre
splitting out of grey everywhere, in the gum forest.

In there for miles, shade track and ironbark slope,
depth casually beginning all around, at a little distance.

Sky sifting, and always a hint of smoke in the light;
you can never reach the heart of the gum forest.

In here is like a great yacht harbour, charmed to leaves,
innumerable tackle, poles wrapped in spattered sail,
or an unknown army in reserve for centuries.

Flooded-gums on creek ground, each tall because of each.
Now a blackbutt in bloom is showering with bees
but warm blood sleeps in the middle of the day.

The witching hour is noon in the gum forest.   .
Foliage builds like a layering splash: ground water
drily upheld in edge-on, wax-rolled, gall-puckered
leaves upon leaves. The shoal life of parrots up there.

Stone footings, trunk-shattered. Non-human lights.
Enormous abandoned machines. The mysteries of the gum forest.

Delight to me, though, at the water-smuggling creeks,
health to me, too, under banksia candles and combs.

A wind is up, rubbing limbs above the bullock roads;
mountains are waves in the ocean of the gum forest.

I go my way, looking back sometimes, looking round me;
singed oils clear my mind, and the pouring sound high up.

Why have I denied the passions of my time? To see
lightning strike upward out of the gum forest.

Rainwater Tank

Empty rings when tapped give tongue,
rings that are tense with water talk:
as he sounds them, ring by rung,
Joe Mitchell's reddened knuckles walk.

The cattledog's head sinks down a notch
and another notch, beside the tank,
and Mitchell's boy, with an old jack-plane,
lifts moustaches from a plank.

From the puddle that the tank has dripped
hens peck glimmerings and uptilt
their heads to shape the quickness down;
petunias live on what gets spilt.

The tankstand spider adds a spittle
thread to her portrait of her soul.
Pencil-grey and stacked like shillings
out of a banker's paper roll

stands the tank, roof-water drinker.
The downpipe stares drought into it.
Briefly the kitchen tap turns on
then off. But the tank says Debit, Debit.

The Future

There is nothing about it. Much science fiction is set there
but is not about it. Prophecy is not about it.
It sways no yarrow stalks. And crystal is a mirror.
Even the man we nailed on a tree for a lookout
said little about it; he told us evil would come.
We see, by convention, a small living distance into it
but even that's a projection. And all our projections
fail to curve where it curves.
                              It is the black hole
out of which no radiation escapes to us.
The commonplace and magnificent roads of our lives
go on some way through cityscape and landscape
or steeply sloping, or scree, into that sheer fall
where everything will be that we have ever sent there,
compacted, spinning – except perhaps us, to see it.
It is said we see the start.
                              But, from here, there's a blindness.
The side-heaped chasm that will swallow all our present
blinds us to the normal sun that may be imagined
shining calmly away on the far side of it, for others
in their ordinary day. A day to which all our portraits,
ideals, revolutions, denim and deshabille
are quaintly heartrending. To see those people is impossible,
to greet them, mawkish. Nonetheless, I begin:
'When I was alive – '
                              and I am turned around
to find myself looking at a cheerful picnic party,
the women decently legless, in muslin and gloves,
the men in beards and weskits, with the long
cheroots and duck trousers of the better sort,
relaxing on a stone verandah. Ceylon, or Sydney.

And as I look, I know they are utterly gone,
each one on his day, with pillow, small bottles, mist,
with all the futures they dreamed or dealt in, going
down to that engulfment everything approaches;
with the man on the tree, they have vanished into the Future.

Immigrant Voyage

My wife came out on the *Goya*
in the mid-year of our century.

In the fogs of that winter
many hundred ships were sounding;
the DP camps were being washed to sea.

The bombsites and the ghettoes
were edging out to Israel,
to Brazil, to Africa, America.

The separating ships were bound away
to the cities of refuge
built for the age of progress.

Hull-down and pouring light
the tithe-barns, the cathedrals
were bearing the old castes away.

★

Pattern-bombed out of babyhood,
Hungarians-become-Swiss,
the children heard their parents:
Argentina? Or Australia?
Less politics, in Australia . . .

Dark Germany, iron frost
and the waiting many weeks
then a small converted warship
under the moon, turning south.

Way beyond the first star
and beyond Cape Finisterre
the fishes and the birds
did eat of their heave-offerings.

★

The *Goya* was a barracks:
mess-queue, spotlights, tower,
crossing the Middle Sea.

In the haunted blue light
that burned nightlong in the sleeping-decks
the tiered bunks were restless
with coughing, demons, territory.

On the Sea of Sweat, the Red Sea,
the flat heat melted even
dulled deference of the injured.
Nordics and Slavonics
paid salt-tax day and night, being
absolved of Europe

but by the Gate of Tears
the barrack was a village
with accordions and dancing
(Fräulein, kennen Sie meinen Rhythmus?)
approaching the southern stars.

★

Those who said Europe
has fallen to the Proles
and the many who said
we are going for the children,

the nouveau poor
and the cheerful shirtsleeve Proles,
the children, who thought
No Smoking signs meant men
mustn't dress for dinner,

those who had hopes
and those who knew that they
were giving up their lives

were becoming the people
who would say, and sometimes urge,
in the English-speaking years:
we came out on the *Goya*.

★

At last, a low coastline,
old horror of Dutch sail-captains.

Behind it, still unknown,
sunburnt farms, strange trees, family jokes
and all the classes of equality.

As it fell away northwards
there was one last week for songs,
for dreaming at the rail,
for beloved meaningless words.

Standing in to Port Phillip
in the salt-grey summer light
the village dissolved
into strained shapes holding luggage;

now they, like the dour
Australians below them, were facing
encounter with the Foreign
where all subtlety fails.

★

Those who, with effort,
with concealment, with silence, had resisted
the collapsed star Death,
who had clawed their families from it,
those crippled by that gravity

were suddenly, shockingly
being loaded aboard lorries:
They say, another camp –
One did not come for this –

As all the refitted
ships stood, oiling, in the Bay,
spectres, furious and feeble,
accompanied the trucks through Melbourne,

resignation, understandings
that cheerful speed dispelled at length.

That first day, rolling north
across the bright savanna,
not yet people, but numbers.
Population. Forebears.

★

Bonegilla, Nelson Bay,
the dry-land barbed wire ships
from which some would never land.

In these, as their parents
learned the Fresh Start music:
physicians nailing crates,
attorneys cleaning trams,
the children had one last
ambiguous summer holiday.

Ahead of them lay
the Deep End of the schoolyard,
tribal testing, tribal soft-drinks,
and learning English fast,
the Wang-Wang language.

Ahead of them, refinements:
thumbs hooked down hard under belts
to repress gesticulation;

ahead of them, epithets:
wog, reffo, Commo Nazi,
things which can be forgotten
but must first be told.

And farther ahead
in the years of the Coffee Revolution
and the Smallgoods Renaissance,
the early funerals:

the misemployed, the unadaptable,
those marked by the Abyss,

friends who came on the *Goya*
in the mid-year of our century.

The Craze Field

These lagoons, these watercourses,
streets of the underworld.
Their water has become the trees that stand along them.

Below root-revetments, in the circles of the water's recession
the ravines seem thronged with a legacy of lily pads.
Earth curls and faintly glistens, scumbled painterly and peeling.

Palates of drought-stilled assonance,
they are cupped flakes of grit, crisps of bottom, dried meniscus
lifted at the edges.

Abstracts realized in slime. Shards of bubble, shrivelled viscose
of clay and stopped life:
the scales of the water snake have gone to grey on this channel.

★

Exfoliate bark of the rain tree, all the outer
plaques have a jostling average size.
It is a kind of fire, the invention of networks.

Water's return, however gradual (and it won't be)
however gentle (it won't be) would not re-lay all seamless
this basal membrane;
it has borne excess of clarity.

This is the lush sheet that overlay the first cities,
the mother-goddess towns, but underlay them first;
this they had for mortar.

Laminar, half detached, these cusps are primal tissue,
foreshadowings of leaf, pottery, palimpsest,
the Dead Lagoon Scrolls.

In this hollow season
everything is perhaps to be recapitulated,
hurriedly, approximately. It is a kind of fire.
Saturate calm is all sprung, in the mother country.

★

The lagoon-bed museums meanwhile have a dizzy stillness
that will reduce, with all the steps that are coming,
to meal, grist, morsels.
Dewfall and birds' feet have nipped, blind noons have nibbled
this mineral matzoh.

The warlike peace-talking young, pacing this dominion
in the beautiful flesh that outdoes their own creations,
might read gnomic fragments:
                              corr   lux   Romant   irit
or fragmentary texts:
    who lose belief in God will not only believe
    in anything. They will bring blood offerings to it.

Bones, snags, seed capsules,
intrinsic in the Martian central pan,
are hidden, in the craze, under small pagoda eaves.

The Grassfire Stanzas

August, and black centres expand on the afternoon paddock.
Dilating on a match in widening margins, they lift
a splintering murmur; they fume out of used-up grass
that's been walked, since summer, into infinite swirled licks.

The man imposing spring here swats with his branch, controlling it:
only small things may come to a head, in this
settlement pattern.

Fretted with small flame, the aspiring islands leave
odd plumes behind. Smuts shower up every thermal
to float down long stairs. Aggregate smoke attracts a kestrel.

Eruption of darkness from far down under roots
is the aspect of these cores, on the undulating farmland;
dense black is withered into web, inside a low singing;
it is dried and loosened, on the surface; it is made weak.

The green feed that shelters beneath its taller death yearly
is unharmed, under new loaf soot. Arriving hawks teeter
and plunge continually, working over the hopping outskirts.

The blackenings are balanced, on a gradient of dryness
in the almost-still air, between dying thinly away
and stripping the whole countryside. Joining, they never gain
more than they lose. They spread away from their high moments.

The man carries smoke wrapped in bark, and keeps applying it
starting new circles. He is burning the passive ocean
around his ark of buildings and his lifeboat water.

It wasn't this man, but it was man, sing the agile
exclamatory birds, who taught them this rapt hunting
(strike! in the updrafts, snap! of hardwood pods).
Humans found the fire here. It is inherent. They learn,
wave after wave of them, how to touch the country.

Sterilizing reed distaffs, the fire edges on to a dam;
it circuits across a cow-track; new surf starts riding outward
and a nippy kestrel feeds from its foot, over cooling mergers.

It's the sun that is touched, and dies in expansion, mincing,
making the round dance, foretelling its future, driving
the frantic lives outwards. The sun that answers the bark tip
is discharged in many little songs, to forestall a symphony.

Cattle come, with stilted bounding calves. They look across the
ripple lines of heat, and shake their armed heads at them;
at random, then, they step over. Grazing smudged black country
they become the beasts of Tartarus. Wavering, moving out over
dung-smouldering ground still covered with its uncovering.

Homage to the Launching-place

Pleasure-craft of the sprung rhythms, bed,
            kindest of quadrupeds,
you are also the unrocking boat
            that moves on silence.

Straining hatchway into this world,
            you sustain our collapses
above earth; guarantor of evolution,
            you are our raised base-line.

Resisting gravity, for us and in us,
            you form a planet-wide
unobtrusive discontinuous platform,
            a layer: the mattressphere,
pretty nearly our highest common level
            (tables may dispute it).

Muscles' sweatprinted solace,
godmother of butt-stubbing dreams,
        you sublimate, Great Vehicle,
all our upright passions;
        midwife of figuring, and design,
you moderate them wisely;
        aiming solitude outwards, at action,
you sigh Think some more. Sleep on it . . .

Solitude. Approaching rest
Time reveals her oscillation
        and narrows into space;
        there is time in that dilation:
        Mansions. Defiles. Continents.
        The living and the greatly living,
        objects that take sides,
        that aren't morally neutral —

you accept my warm absence
        there, as you will accept,
one day, my cooling presence.

        I loved you from the first, bed,
doorway out of this world;
        above your inner springs
I learned to dig my own.

        Primly dressed, linen-collared one,
you look so still, for your speed,
        shield that carries us to the fight
        and bears us from it.

First Essay on Interest

Not usury, but interest. The cup slowed in mid-raise,
the short whistle, hum, the little forwards shift
mark our intake of that non-physical breath

which the lungs mimic sharply, to cancel the gap in pressure
left by our self vanishing into its own alert –
A blink returns us to self, that intimate demeanour

self-repairing as a bow-wave. What we have received
is the ordinary mail of the otherworld, wholly common,
not postmarked divine; no one refuses delivery,

not even the eagle, her face fixed at heavy Menace:
I have juices to sort the relevant from the irrelevant;
even her gaze may tilt left, askance, aloof, right,
fixing a still unknown. Delaying huge flight.

Interest. Mild and inherent with fire as oxygen,
it is a sporadic inhalation. We can live long days
under its surface, breathing material air

then something catches, is itself. Intent and special silence.
This is interest, that blinks our interests out
and alone permits their survival, by relieving

us of their gravity, for a timeless moment;
that centres where it points, and points to centring,
that centres us where it points, and reflects our centre.

It is a form of love. The everyday shines through it
and patches of time. But it does not mingle with these;
it wakens only for each trace in them of the Beloved.

And this breath of interest is non-rhythmical;
it is human to obey, humane to be wary of rhythm
as tainted by the rallies, as marching with the snare drum.
The season of interest is not fixed in the calendar cycle;

it pulls towards acute dimensions. Death is its intimate.
When that Holland of cycles, the body, veers steeply downhill
interest retreats from the face; it ceases to instill
and fade, like breath; it becomes a vivid steady state

that registers every grass-blade seen on the way,
the long combed grain in the steps, free insects flying;
it stands aside from your panic, the wracked disarray;
it behaves as if it were the part of you not dying.

Affinity of interest with extremity
seems to distil to this polar disaffinity
that suggests the beloved is not death, but rather
what our death has hidden. Which may be this world.

The Fishermen at South Head

They have walked out as far as they can go on the prow of the
    continent,
on the undercut white sandstone, the bowsprits of the towering
    headland.
They project their long light canes
or raise them up to check and string, like quiet archers.
Between casts they hold them couched,
a finger on the line, two fingers on a cigarette, the reel cocked.

They watch the junction of smooth blue with far matt-shining
    blue,
the join where clouds enter,
or they watch the wind-shape of their nylon
bend like a sail's outline
south towards, a mile away, the city's floating gruel
of gull-blown effluent.

Sometimes they glance north, at the people on that calf-coloured
    edge
lower than theirs, where the suicides come by taxi
and stretchers are winched up
later, under raining lights
but mostly their eyes stay level with the land–and–ocean glitter.

Where they stand, atop the centuries
of strata, they don't look down much
but feel through their tackle the talus-eddying
and tidal detail of that huge simple pulse
in the rock and their bones.

Through their horizontal poles they divine the creatures of ocean:
a touch, a dip, and a busy winding death gets started;

hands will turn for minutes, rapidly,
before, still opening its pitiful doors, the victim
dawns above the rim, and is hoisted in a flash above the suburbs
– or before the rod flips, to stand
trailing sworn-at gossamer.

On that highest dreadnought scarp, where the terra cotta
waves of bungalows stop, suspended at sky,
the hunters stand apart.
They encourage one another, at a distance, not by talk

but by being there, by unhooking now and then
a twist of silver for the creel, by a vaguely mutual
zodiac of cars TV windcheaters.
Braced, casual normality. Anything unshared,
a harlequin mask, a painted wand flourished at the sun,
would anger them. It is serious to be with humans.

View of Sydney, Australia, from Gladesville Road Bridge

There's the other great arch eastward, with its hanging highways;
the headlands and horizons of packed suburb, white among
   bisque-fired; odd smokes rising;
there's Warrang, the flooded valley, that is now the ship-chained
   Harbour,
recurrent everywhere, with its azure and its grains;
ramped parks, bricked containers,
verandahs successive around walls,
and there's the central highrise, multi-storey, the twenty-year
   countdown,
the new city standing on its haze above the city.

   Ingots of sheer
   affluence poles
   bomb-drawing grid
   of columnar profit
   piecrust and scintillant
   tunnels in the sky
   high window printouts
   repeat their lines
   repeat their lines
   credit conductors
   repeat their lines
   bar graphs on blue
   glass tubes of boom
   in concrete wicker
   each trade Polaris
   government Agena
   fine print insurrected
   tall drinks on a tray

All around them is the old order: brewery brick terrace hospital
horrible workplace; the scale of the tramway era,
the peajacket era, the age of the cliff-repeating woolstores.
South and west lie the treeless suburbs, a mulch of faded flags,
north and partly east, the built-in paradise forest.

Quintets for Robert Morley

Is it possible that hyper-
ventilating up Parnassus
I have neglected to pay tribute
to the Stone Age aristocracy?
    I refer to the fat.

We were probably the earliest
civilized, and civilizing, humans,
the first to win the leisure,
sweet boredom, life-enhancing sprawl
    that require style.

Tribesfolk spared us and cared for us
for good reasons. Our reasons.
As age's counterfeits, forerunners of the city,
we survived, and multiplied. Out of self-defence
    we invented the Self.

It's likely we also invented some of love,
much of fertility (see the Willensdorf Venus)
parts of theology (divine feasting, Unmoved Movers)
likewise complexity, stateliness, the ox-cart
    and self-deprecation.

Not that the lists of pugnacity are bare
of stout fellows. Ask a Sumo.
Warriors taunt us still, and fear us:
in heroic war, we are apt to be the specialists
    and the generals.

But we do better in peacetime. For ourselves
we would spare the earth. We were the first moderns
after all, being like the Common Man
disqualified from tragedy. Accessible to shame, though,
    subtler than the tall,

we make reasonable rulers.
Never trust a lean meritocracy
nor the leader who has been lean;
only the lifelong big have the knack of wedding
    greatness with balance.

Never wholly trust the fat man
who lurks in the lean achiever
and in the defeated, yearning to get out.
He has not been through our initiations,
    he lacks the light feet.

Our having life abundantly
is equivocal, Robert, in hot climates
where the hungry watch us. I lack the light step then
    too.
How many of us, I wonder, walk those streets
    in terrible disguise?

So much climbing, on a spherical world;
had Newton not been a mere beginner at gravity
he might have asked how the apple got up there
in the first place. And so might have discerned
    an ampler physics.

Equanimity

Nests of golden porridge shattered in the silky-oak trees,
cobs and crusts of it, their glory-box;
the jacarandas' open violet immensities
mirrored flat on the lawns,
weighted by sprinklers; birds, singly and in flocks
hopping over the suburb, eating, as birds do, in detail
and paying their peppercorns;
talk of 'the good life' tangles love with will

however; if we mention it, there is more to say:
the droughty light, for example, at telephone-wire
height above the carports, not the middle-ground
distilling news-photograph light of a smoggy Wednesday,
but that light of the north-west wind, hung on the sky
like the haze above cattleyards;

hungry mountain birds, too, drifting in for food, with the sound
of moist gullies about them, and the sound of the pinch-bar;
we must hear the profoundly unwished
garble of a neighbours' quarrel, and see repeatedly
the face we saw near the sportswear shop today
in which mouth-watering and tears couldn't be distinguished.

Fire-prone place-names apart
there is only love; there are no Arcadias.
Whatever its variants of meat-cuisine, worship, divorce,
human order has at heart
an equanimity. Quite different from inertia, it's a place
where the churchman's not defensive, the indignant aren't on the
    qui vive,
the loser has lost interest, the accountant is truant to remorse,
where the farmer has done enough struggling-to-survive
for one day, and the artist rests from theory —
where all are, in short, off the high comparative horse
of their identity.
Almost beneath notice, as attainable as gravity, it is
a continuous recovering moment. Pity the high madness
that misses it continually, ranging without rest between
assertion and unconsciousness,
the sort that makes Hell seem a height of evolution.
Through the peace beneath effort
(even within effort: quiet air between the bars of our attention)
comes unpurchased lifelong plenishment;
Christ spoke to people most often on this level
especially when they chattered about kingship and the Romans;
all holiness speaks from it.

From the otherworld of action and media, this
interleaved continuing plane is hard to focus:
we are looking into the light –
it makes some smile, some grimace.
More natural to look at the birds about the street, their life
that is greedy, pinched, courageous and prudential
as any on these bricked tree-mingled miles of settlement,
to watch the unceasing on-off
grace that attends their nearly every movement,
the same grace moveless in the shapes of trees
and complex in our selves and fellow walkers: we see it's indivisible
and scarcely willed. That it lights us from the incommensurable
we sometimes glimpse, from being trapped in the point
(bird minds and ours are so pointedly visual):
a field all foreground, and equally all background,
like a painting of equality. Of infinite detailed extent
like God's attention. Where nothing is diminished by perspective.

Shower

From the metal poppy
this good blast of trance
arriving as shock, private cloudburst blazing down,
worst in a boarding-house greased tub, or a barrack with
    competitions,
best in a stall, this enveloping passion of Australians:
tropics that sweat for you, torrent that braces with its heat,
inflames you with its chill, action sauna, inverse bidet,
sleek vertical coruscating ghost of your inner river,
reminding all your fluids, streaming off your points, awakening
the tacky soap to blossom and ripe autumn, releasing the
    squeezed gardens,
smoky valet smoothing your impalpable overnight pyjamas off,
pillar you can step through, force-field absolving love's efforts,
nicest yard of the jogging track, speeding aeroplane minutely
steered with two controls, or trimmed with a knurled wheel.
Some people like to still this energy and lie in it,

stirring circles with their pleasure in it – but my delight's that toga
worn on either or both shoulders, fluted drapery, silk whispering
    to the tiles
with its spiralling frothy hem continuous round the gurgle-hole;
this ecstatic partner, dreamy to dance in slow embrace with
after factory-floor rock, or even to meet as Lot's abstracted
merciful wife on a rusty ship in dog latitudes,
sweetest dressing of the day in the dusty bush, this persistent
time-capsule of unwinding, this nimble straight wellwisher.
Only in England is its name an unkind word;
only in Europe is it enjoyed by telephone.

Two Poems in Memory of My Mother,
Miriam Murray née Arnall

Born 23.5.1915, Died 19.4.1951

Weights

Not owning a cart, my father
in the drought years was a bowing
green hut of cattle feed, moving,
or gasping under cream cans. No weight
would he let my mother carry.

Instead, she wielded handles
in the kitchen and dairy, singing often,
gave saucepan-boiled injections
with her ward-sister skill, nursed neighbours,
scorned gossips, ran committees.

She gave me her factual tone,
her facial bones, her will,
not her beautiful voice
but her straightness and her clarity.

I did not know back then
nor for many years what it was,
after me, she could not carry.

Midsummer Ice

Remember how I used
to carry ice in from the road
for the ice chest, half running,
the white rectangle clamped in bare hands
the only utter cold
in all those summer paddocks?

How, swaying, I'd hurry it inside
en bloc and watering, with the butter
and the wrapped bread precarious on top of it?
'Poor Leslie,' you would say,
'your hands are cold as charity – '
You made me take the barrow
but uphill it was heavy.

We'd no tongs, and a bag
would have soaked and bumped, off balance.
I loved to eat the ice,
chip it out with the butcher knife's grey steel.
It stopped good things rotting
and it had a strange comb at its heart,
a splintered horizon rife with zero pearls.

But you don't remember.
A doorstep of numbed creek water the colour of tears
but you don't remember.
I will have to die before you remember.

Machine Portraits with Pendant Spaceman

for Valerie

The bulldozer stands short as a boot on its heel-high ripple soles;
it has toecapped stumps aside all day, scuffed earth and trampled
   rocks
making a hobnailed dyke downstream of raw clay shoals.
Its work will hold water. The man who bounced high on the box
seat, exercising levers, would swear a full frontal orthodox
oath to that. First he shaved off the grizzled scrub
with that front-end safety razor supplied by the school of hard knocks

then he knuckled down and ground his irons properly; they
   copped many a harsh rub.
At knock-off time, spilling thunder, he surfaced like a sub.

★

Speaking of razors, the workshop amazes with its strop,
its elapsing leather drive-belt angled to the slapstick flow
of fast work in the Chaplin age; tightened, it runs like syrup,
streams like a mill-sluice, fiddles like a glazed virtuoso.
With the straitlaced summary cut of Sam Brownes long ago
it is the last of the drawn lash and bullocking muscle
left in engineering. It's where the panther leaping, his swift shadow
and all such free images turned plastic. Here they dwindle, dense
   with oil,
like a skein between tough factory hands, pulley and diesel.

★

Shaking in slow low flight, with its span of many jets,
the combine seeder at nightfall swimming over flat land
is a style of machinery we'd imagined for the fictional planets:
in the high glassed cabin, above vapour-pencilling floodlights, a
   hand,
gloved against the cold, hunts along the medium-wave band
for company of Earth voices; it crosses speech garble music –
the Brandenburg Conch the Who the Illyrian High Command –

as seed wheat in the hoppers shakes down, being laced into the thick
night-dampening plains soil, and the stars waver out and stick.

★

Flags and a taut fence discipline the mountain pasture
where giant upturned mushrooms gape mildly at the sky
catching otherworld pollen. Poppy-smooth or waffle-ironed,
    each armature
distils wild and white sound. These, Earth's first antennae
tranquilly angled outwards, to a black, not a gold infinity,
swallow the millionfold numbers that print out as a risen
glorious Apollo. They speak control to satellites in high
bursts of algorithm. And some of them are tuned to win
answers to fair questions, viz. What is the Universe in?

★

How many metal-bra and trumpet-flaring film extravaganzas
underlie the progress of the space shuttle's Ground Transporter
    Vehicle
across macadam-surfaced Florida? Atop oncreeping house-high
    panzers,
towering drydock and ocean-liner decks, there perches a gridiron
    football
field in gradual motion; it is the god-platform; it sustains the bridal
skyscraper of liquid Cool, and the rockets borrowed from the
    Superman
and the bricked aeroplane of Bustout-and-return, all vertical,

conjoined and myth-huge, approaching the starred gantry where
    human
lightning will crack, extend, and vanish upwards from this caravan.

★

    Gold-masked, the foetal warrior
    unslipping on a flawless floor,
    I backpack air; my life machine
    breathes me head-Earthwards, speaks the Choctaw

51

of tech-talk that earths our discipline –
but the home world now seems outside-in;
I marvel that here background's so fore
and sheathe my arms in the unseen
a dream in images unrecalled
from any past takes me   I soar
at the heart of fall on a drifting line
this is the nearest I have been
to oneness with the everted world
the unsinking leap   the stone unfurled

★

In a derelict village picture show I will find a projector,
dust-matted, but with film in its drum magazines, and the lens
mysteriously clean. The film will be called *Insensate Violence*,
no plot, no characters, just shoot burn scream beg claw
bayonet trample brains – I will hit the reverse switch then, in
    conscience,
and the thing will run backwards, unlike its coeval the
    machine-gun;

blood will unspill, fighters lift and surge apart; horror will be
    undone
and I will come out to a large town, bright parrots round the
    saleyard pens
and my people's faces healed of a bitter sophistication.

★

The more I act, the stiller I become;
the less I'm lit, the more spellbound my crowd;
I accept all colours, and with a warming hum
I turn them white and hide them in a cloud.
To give long life is a power I'm allowed
by my servant, Death. I am what you can't sell
at the world's end – and if you're still beetle-browed
try some of my treasures: an adult bird in its shell
or a pink porker in his own gut, Fritz the Abstract Animal.

★

No riddles about a crane. This one drops a black clanger on cars
and the palm of its four-thumbed steel hand is a raptor of
    wrecked tubing;
the ones up the highway hoist porridgy concrete, long spars
and the local skyline; whether raising aloft on a string
bizarre workaday angels, or letting down a rotating
man on a sphere, these machines are inclined to maintain
a peace like world war, in which we turn over everything
to provide unceasing victories. Now the fluent lines stop, and strain
engrosses this tower on the frontier of junk, this crane.

★

Before a landscape sprouts those giant stepladders that pump oil
or before far out iron mosquitoes attach to the sea
there is this sortilege with phones that plug into mapped soil,
the odd gelignite bump to shake trucks, paper scribbling out serially
as men dial Barrier Reefs long enfolded beneath the geology
or listen for black Freudian beaches; they seek a miles-wide pustular
rock dome of pure Crude, a St Paul's-in-profundis. There are many
wrong numbers on the geophone, but it's brought us some
    distance, and by car.
Every machine has been love and a true answer.

★

Not a high studded ship boiling cauliflower under her keel
nor a ghost in bootlaced canvas – just a length of country road
afloat between two shores, winding wet wire rope reel-to-reel,
dismissing romance sternwards. Six cars and a hay truck are her load
plus a thoughtful human cast which could, in some dramatic
    episode,
become a world. All machines in the end join God's creation
growing bygone, given, changeless – but a river ferry has its
    timeless mode
from the grinding reedy outset; it enforces contemplation.
We arrive. We traverse depth in thudding silence. We go on.

The Hypogeum

Below the moveable gardens of this shopping centre
down concrete ways
                    to a level of rainwater,
a black lake glimmering among piers, electric lighted,
windless, of no depth.
                    Rare shafts of daylight
waver at their base. As the water is shaken, the few
cars parked down here seem to rock. In everything
there strains that silent crash, that reverberation
which persists in concrete.
                    The cardboard carton
Lorenzo's Natural Flavour Italian Meat Balls has foundered
into a wet ruin. Dutch Cleanser is propped at a high
featureless wall. Self-raising Flour is still floating
and supermarket trolleys hang their inverse harps,
silver leaking from them.
                    What will help the informally religious
to endure peace? Surface water dripping into
this underworld makes now a musical blip,
now rings from nowhere.
                    Young people descending the ramp
pause at the water's brink, banging their voices.

Second Essay on Interest: The Emu

Weathered blond as a grass tree, a huge Beatles haircut
raises an alert periscope and stares out
over scrub. Her large olivine eggs click
oilily together; her lips of noble plastic
clamped in their expression, her head-fluff a stripe
worn mohawk style, she bubbles her pale-blue windpipe:
the emu, *Dromaius novaehollandiae*,
whose stand-in on most continents is an antelope,

looks us in both eyes with her one eye
and her other eye, dignified courageous hump,
feather-swaying condensed camel, Swift Courser of New Holland.

Knees backward in toothed three-way boots, you stand,
Dinewan, proud emu, common as the dust
in your sleeveless cloak, returning our interest.
Your shield of fashion's wobbly: You're Quaint, you're Native,
even somewhat Bygone. You may be let live –
but beware: the blank zones of Serious disdain
are often carte blanche to the darkly human.
Europe's boats on their first strange shore looked humble
but, Mass over, men started renaming the creatures.
Worship turned to interest and had new features.
Now only life survives, if it's made remarkable.

Heraldic bird, our protection is a fable
made of space and neglect. We're remarkable and not;
we're the ordinary discovered on a strange planet.
Are you Early or Late, in the history of birds
which doesn't exist, and is deeply ancient?
My kinships, too, are immemorial and recent,
like my country, which abstracts yours in words.
This distillate of mountains is finely branched, this plain
expanse of dour delicate lives, where the rain,
shrouded slab on the west horizon, is a corrugated revenant
settling its long clay-tipped plumage in a hatching descent.

Rubberneck, stepped sister, I see your eye on our jeep's load.
I think your story is, when you were offered
the hand of evolution, you gulped it. Forefinger and thumb
project from your face, but the weighing palm is inside you
collecting the bottletops, nails, wet cement that you famously
    swallow,
your passing muffled show, your serially private museum.
Some truths are now called *trivial*, though. Only God approves them.
Some humans who disdain them make a kind of weather
which, when it grows overt and widespread, we call *war*.
There we make death trivial and awesome, by rapid turns about,
we conscript it to bless us, force-feed it to squeeze the drama out;

indeed we imprison and torture death – this part is called *peace* –
we offer it murder like mendicants, begging for significance.
You rustle dreams of pardon, not fleeing in your hovercraft style,
not gliding fast with zinc-flaked legs dangling, feet making high-
    tensile
seesawing impacts. Wasteland parent, barely edible dignitary,
the disinterested spotlight of the lords of interest
and gowned nobles of ennui is a torch of vivid arrest
and blinding after-darkness. But you hint it's a brigand sovereignty
after the steady extents of God's common immortality
whose image is daylight detail, aggregate, in process yet plumb
to the everywhere focus of one devoid of boredom.

A Retrospect of Humidity

All the air conditioners now slacken
their hummed carrier wave. Once again
we've served our three months with remissions
in the steam and dry iron of this seaboard.
In jellied glare, through the nettle-rash season,
we've watched the sky's fermenting laundry
portend downpours. Some came, and steamed away,
and we were clutched back into the rancid
saline midnights of orifice weather,
to damp grittiness and wiping off the air.

Metaphors slump irritably together in
the muggy weeks. Shark and jellyfish shallows
become suburbs where you breathe a fat towel;
babies burst like tomatoes with discomfort
in the cotton-wrapped pointing street markets;
the lycra-bulging surf drips from non-swimmers
miles from shore, and somehow includes soil.
Skins, touching, soak each other. Skin touching
any surface wets that and itself
in a kind of mutual digestion.
Throbbing heads grow lianas of nonsense.

It's our annual visit to the latitudes
of rice, kerosene and resignation,
an averted, temporary visit
unrelated, for most, to the attitudes
of festive northbound jets gaining height –
closer, for some few, to the memory
of ulcers scraped with a tin spoon
or sweated faces bowing before dry
where the flesh is worn inside out,
all the hunger-organs clutched in rank nylon,
by those for whom exhaustion is spirit:

an intrusive, heart–narrowing season
at this far southern foot of the monsoon.
As the kleenex flower, the hibiscus
drops its browning wads, we forget
annually, as one forgets a sickness.
The stifling days will never come again,
not now that we've seen the first sweater
tugged down on the beauties of division
and inside the rain's millions, a risen
loaf of cat on a cool night verandah.

Flowering Eucalypt in Autumn

That slim creek out of the sky
the dried-blood western gum tree
is all stir in its high reaches:

its strung haze-blue foliage is dancing
points down in breezy mobs, swapping
pace and place in an all-over sway

retarded en masse by crimson blossom.
Bees still at work up there tack
around their exploded furry likeness

and the lawn underneath's a napped rug
of eyelash drift, of blooms flared
like a sneeze in a redhaired nostril,

minute urns, pinch-sized rockets
knocked down by winds, by night-creaking
fig-squirting bats, or the daily

parrot gang with green pocketknife wings.
Bristling food for tough delicate
raucous life, each flower comes

as a spray in its own turned vase,
a taut starburst, honeyed model
of the tree's fragrance crisping in your head.

When the Japanese plum tree
was shedding in spring, we speculated
there among the drizzling petals

what kind of exquisitely precious
artistic bloom might be gendered
in a pure ethereal compost

of petals potted as they fell.
From unpetalled gum-debris
we know what is grown continually,

a tower of fabulous swish tatters,
a map hoisted upright, a crusted
riverbed with up-country show towns.

The Chimes of Neverwhere

How many times did the Church prevent war?
Who knows? Those wars did not occur.

The neither state of Neverwhere
is hard to place as near or far
since all things that didn't take place are there
and things that have lost the place they took:

Herr Hitler's buildings, King James' cigar,
the happiness of Armenia,
the Abelard children, the Manchus' return
are there with the Pictish Grammar Book.

The girl who returned your dazzled look
and the mornings you might have woke to her
are your waterbed in Neverwhere.
There shine the dukes of Australia

and all the great poems that never were
quite written, and every balked invention.
There too are the Third AIF and its war
in which I and boys my age were killed

more pointlessly with each passing year,
but there too half the works of sainthood are,
the enslavements, tortures, rapes, despair
deflected by them from the actual

to rain on the human–sacrifice drum
which millions never have to hear
beating for them in Neverwhere.

The Smell of Coal Smoke

John Brown, glowing far and down,
wartime Newcastle was a brown town,
handrolled cough and cardigan, rain on paving bricks,
big smoke to a four-year-old from the green sticks.
Train city, mother's city, coming on dark,
Japanese shell holes awesome in a park,
electric light and upstairs, encountered first that day,
sailors and funny ladies in Jerry's Fish Café.

It is always evening on those earliest trips,
raining through the tram wires where blue glare rips
across the gaze of wonderment and leaves thrilling tips.

The steelworks' vast roofed debris unrolling falls
of smoky stunning orange, its eye-hurting slump walls
mellow to lounge interiors, cut pile and curry-brown
with the Pears-Soap-smelling fire and a sense of ships
mourning to each other below in the town.

This was my mother's childhood and her difference,
her city-brisk relations who valued Sense
talking strike and colliery, engineering, fowls and war,
Brown's grit and miners breathing it, years before
as I sat near the fire, raptly touching coal,
its blockage, slick yet dusty, prisms massed and dense
in the iron scuttle, its hammered bulky roll
into the glaring grate to fracture and shoal,

its chips you couldn't draw with on the cement
made it a stone, tar crockery, different –
and I had three grandparents, while others had four:
where was my mother's father, never called Poor?
In his tie and his Vauxhall that had a boat bow
driving up the Coalfields, but where was he now?
Coal smoke as much as gum trees now had a tight scent
to summon deep brown evenings of the Japanese war,

to conjure gaslit pub yards, their razory frisson
and sense my dead grandfather, the Grafton Cornishman,
rising through the night schools by the pressure in his chest
as his lungs creaked like mahogany with the grains of John Brown.
His city, mother's city, at its starriest
as swearing men with doctors' bags streamed by toward the docks
past the smoke-frothing wooden train that would take us home
    soon
with our day-old Henholme chickens peeping in their box.

Time Travel

for Daniel

To revisit the spitfire world
of the duel, you put on a suit
of white body armour, a helmet
like an insect's composite eye
and step out like a space walker
under haloed lights, trailing a cord.

Descending, with nodding foil in hand
towards the pomander-and-cravat sphere
you meet the Opponent, for this journey
can only be accomplished by a pair
who semaphore and swap quick respect
before they set about their joint effect

which is making zeroes and serifs so
swiftly and with such sprung variety
that the long steels skid, clatter, zing,
switch, batter, bite, kiss and ring
in the complex rhythms of that society
with its warrior snare of comme il faut

that has you facing a starched beau
near stable walls on a misty morning,
striking, seeking the surrender in him,
the pedigree-flaw through which to pin him,
he probing for your own braggadocio,
confusion, ennui or inner fawning –

Seconds, holding stakes and cloths, look grim
and surge a step. Exchanges halt
for one of you stands, ageing horribly,
collapses, drowning from an entry
of narrow hurt. The other gulps hot chocolate
a trifle fast, but talking nonchalant –

a buzzer sounds. Heads are tucked
under arms, and you and he swap
curt nods in a more Christian century.

The Dark

The last interior is darkness. Befuddled past-midnight
fear, testing each step like deep water, that when you open
the eventual refrigerator, cold but no light will envelop you.
Bony hurts that persuade you the names of your guides now
are balance, and gravity. You can fall up things, but not far.
A stopping, teeming caution. As of prey. The dark is arbitrary
delivering wheeled smashes, murmurings, something that scuttled,
doorjambs without a switch. The dark has no subject matter
but is alive with theory. Its best respites are: no surprises.
Nothing touching you. Or panic-stilling chance embraces.
Darkness is the cloth for pained eyes, and lovely in colour,
splendid in the lungs of great singers. Also the needed matrix
of constellations, flaring Ginzas, desert moons, apparent snow,
verandah–edged night rain. Dark is like that: all productions.
Almost nothing there is caused, or has results. Dark is all one
    interior
permitting only inner life. Concealing what will seize it.

Flood Plains on the Coast Facing Asia

Hitching blur to a caged propeller
with its motor racket swelling
barroom to barrage, our aluminium
airboat has crossed the black coffee
lagoon and swum out onto
one enormous crinkling green.
Now like a rocket loudening
to liftoff, it erects the earsplitting
wigwam we must travel in
everywhere here, and starts skimming
at speed on the never-never
meadows of the monsoon wetland.

Birds lift, scattering before us
over the primeval irrigation,
leaf-running jacanas, twin-boomed
with supplicant bare feet for tails;
knob-headed magpie geese
row into the air ahead of us;
waterlilies lean away, to go
under as we overrun them
and resurrect behind us.
We leave at most a darker green
trace on the universal glittering
and, waterproof in cream and blue,
waterlilies on their stems, circling.

Our shattering car
crossing exposed and seeping spaces
brings us to finely stinking places,
yet whatever riceless paddies
we reach, of whatever grass,
there is always sheeting spray
underhull for our passage;
and the Intermediate Egret leaps
aloft out of stagnant colours

and many a double-barrelled crossbow
shoots vegetable breath emphatically
from the haunts of flaking buffalo;
water glinting everywhere, like ice,
we traverse speeds humans once reached
in such surroundings mainly
as soldiers, in the tropic wars.

At times, we fold our windtunnel
away, in its blackened steel sail
and sit, for talk and contemplation.
For instance, off the deadly islet,
a swamp–surrounded sandstone knoll
split, cabled, commissured
with fig trees' python roots.
Watched by distant plateau cliffs
stitched millennially in every crevice
with the bark-entubed dead
we do not go ashore.
Those hills are ancient stone gods
just beginning to be literature.

We release again the warring sound
of our peaceful tour, and go sledding
headlong through mounded paperbark
copses, on reaches of maroon
grit, our wake unravelling
over green curd where logs lie digesting
and over the breast-lifting deeps
of the file snake, whom the women here
tread on, scoop up, clamp head-first in their teeth
and jerk to death, then carry home as meat.

Loudest without speech, we shear
for miles on the paddock of nymphaeas
still hoisting up the paired pied geese,
their black goslings toddling below them.
We, a family with baby and two friends,
one swift metal skin above the food-chains,
the extensible wet life-chains of which

our civility and wake are one stretch,
the pelicans circling over us another
and the cat-napping peace of the secure,
of eagles, lions and two-year-old George
asleep beneath his pink linen hat as
we enter domains of flowering lotus.

In our propeller's stiffened silence
we stand up among scalloped leaves
that are flickering for hundreds of acres
on their deeper water. The lotus
prove a breezy nonhuman gathering
of this planet, with their olive-studded
rubbery cocktail glasses, loose carmine roses,
salmon buds like the five-fingertips-joined
gesture of summation, of *ecco*!
waist-high around us in all their greenery
on yeasty frog water. We receive this
sidelong, speaking our wiry language
in which so many others ghost and flicker.

We discuss Leichhardt's party and their qualities
when, hauling the year 1845
through here, with spearheads embedded in it,
their bullock drays reached and began skirting
this bar of literal water
after the desert months which had been
themselves a kind of swimming,
a salt undersea plodding, monster-haunted
with odd very pure surfacings.
We also receive, in drifts of calm
hushing, which fret the baby boy,
how the fuzzed gold innumerable cables
by which this garden hangs skyward
branch beneath the surface, like dreams.

The powerful dream of being harmless,
the many chains snapped and stretched hard for that:
both shimmer behind our run back
toward the escarpments where stallion-eyed

Lightning lives, who'd shiver all heights
down and make of the earth
one oozing, feeding peneplain.
Unprotected Lightning: there are his wild horses
and brolgas, and far heron not rising.
Suddenly we run over a crocodile.
On an unlilied deep, bare even
of minute water fern, it leaped out,
surged man-swift straight under us. We ran over it.
We circle back. Unhurt, it floats, peering
from each small eye turret, then annuls
buoyancy and merges subtly under,
swollen leathers becoming gargoyle stone,
chains of contour, with pineapple abdomen.

The Dream of Wearing Shorts Forever

To go home and wear shorts forever
in the enormous paddocks, in that warm climate,
adding a sweater when winter soaks the grass,

to camp out along the river bends
for good, wearing shorts, with a pocketknife,
a fishing line and matches,

or there where the hills are all down, below the plain,
to sit around in shorts at evening
on the plank verandah –

If the cardinal points of costume
are Robes, Tat, Rig and Scunge,
where are shorts in this compass?

They are never Robes
as other bareleg outfits have been:
the toga, the kilt, the lava-lava
the Mahatma's cotton dhoti;

archbishops and field marshals
at their ceremonies never wear shorts.
The very word
means underpants in North America.

Shorts can be Tat,
Land-Rovering bush-environmental tat,
socio-political ripped-and-metal-stapled tat,
solidarity-with-the-Third-World tat tvam asi,

likewise track-and-field shorts worn to parties
and the further humid, modelling negligée
of the Kingdom of Flaunt,
that unchallenged aristocracy.

More plainly climatic, shorts
are farmers' rig, leathery with salt and bonemeal,
are sailors' and branch bankers' rig,
the crisp golfing style
of our youngest male National Costume.

Mostly loosely, they are Scunge,
ancient Bengal bloomers or moth-eaten hot pants
worn with a former shirt,
feet, beach sand, hair
and a paucity of signals.

Scunge, which is real negligée
housework in a swimsuit, pyjamas worn all day,
is holiday, is freedom from ambition.
Scunge makes you invisible
to the world and yourself.

The entropy of costume,
scunge can get you conquered by more vigorous cultures
and help you to notice it less.

Satisfied ambition, defeat, true unconcern,
the wish and the knack for self-forgetfulness
all fall within the scunge ambit
wearing board shorts or similar;
it is a kind of weightlessness.

Unlike public nakedness, which in Westerners
is deeply circumstantial, relaxed as exam time,
artless and equal as the corsetry of a hussar regiment,

shorts and their plain like
are an angelic nudity,
spirituality with pockets!
A double updraft as you drop from branch to pool!

Ideal for getting served last
in shops of the temperate zone
they are also ideal for going home, into space,
into time, to farm the mind's Sabine acres
for product or subsistence.

Now that everyone who yearned to wear long pants
has essentially achieved them,
long pants, which have themselves been underwear
repeatedly, and underground more than once,
it is time perhaps to cherish the culture of shorts,

to moderate grim vigour
with the knobble of bare knees,
to cool bareknuckle feet in inland water,
slapping flies with a book on solar wind
or a patient bare hand, beneath the cadjiput trees,

to be walking meditatively
among green timber, through the grassy forest
towards a calm sea
and looking across to more of that great island
and the further topics.

At the Aquatic Carnival

Two racing boats seen from the harmonic railing
of this road bridge quit their wakes,
plane above their mirroring shield-forms
and bash the river, flat out, their hits batts of appliqué
violently spreading, their turnings eiderdown
abolishing translucency before the frieze of people,
and rolled-over water comes out to the footings of the carnival.

Even up drinking coffee-and-froth in the town
prodigious sound rams through arcades and alleyways
and burrs in our teeth, beneath the slow nacelle
of a midsummer ceiling fan.
No wonder pelicans vanish from their river at these times.
How, we wonder, does that sodden undersized one
who hangs around the Fish Co-op get by?
The pert wrymouth with the twisted upper beak.

It cannot pincer prey, or lid its lower scoop,
and so lives on guts, mucking in with the others
who come and go. For it to leave would be death.
Its trouble looks like a birth defect, not an injury,
and raises questions.
There are poetics would require it to be pecked
to death by fellow pelicans, or kids to smash it with a stick,
preserving a hard cosmos.

In fact it came with fellow pelicans, parents maybe,
and has been around for years. Humans who feed it
are sentimental, perhaps – but what to say
of humans who refused to feed a lame bird?
Nature is not human-hearted. But it is one flesh
or we could not imagine it. And we could not eat.

Nature is not human-hearted. So the animals
come to man, at first in their extremity:
the wild scrub turkeys entering farms in drought-time,
the done fox suddenly underfoot among dog-urgers
(that frantic compliment, that prayer never granted by dogs)
or the shy birds perching on human shoulders and trucks
when the mountains are blotted out in fiery dismemberment.

The Sleepout

Childhood sleeps in a verandah room
in an iron bed close to the wall
where the winter over the railing
swelled the blind on its timber boom

and splinters picked lint off warm linen
and the stars were out over the hill;
then one wall of the room was forest
and all things in there were to come.

Breathings climbed up on the verandah
when dark cattle rubbed at a corner
and sometimes dim towering rain stood
for forest, and the dry cave hunched woollen.

Inside the forest was lamplit
along tracks to a starry creek bed
and beyond lay the never-fenced country,
its full billabongs all surrounded

by animals and birds, in loud crustings,
and something kept leaping up amongst them.
And out there, to kindle whenever
dark found it, hung the daylight moon.

Louvres

In the banana zone, in the poinciana tropics
reality is stacked on handsbreadth shelving,
open and shut, it is ruled across with lines
as in a gleaming gritty exercise book.

The world is seen through a cranked or levered
weatherboarding of explosive glass
angled floor-to-ceiling. Horizons which metre
the dazzling outdoors into green-edged couplets.

In the louvred latitudes
children fly to sleep in triplanes, and
cool nights are eerie with retracting flaps.

Their houses stand aloft among bougainvillea,
covered bridges that lead down a shining hall
from love to mystery to breakfast,
from babyhood to moving-out day

and visitors shimmer up in columnar gauges
to touch lives lived behind gauze
in a lantern of inventory,
slick vector geometries glossing the months of rain.

There, nudity is dizzily cubist, and directions
have to include: stage left, add an inch of breeze
or: enter a glistening tendril.

Every building of jinked and slatted ledges
is at times a squadron of inside-out
helicopters, humming with rotor fans.

For drinkers under cyclonic pressure, such
a house can be a bridge of scythes –
groundlings scuffing by stop only for dénouements.

But everyone comes out on platforms of command
to survey cloudy flame-trees, the plain of streets, the future:
only then descending to the level of affairs

and if these things are done in the green season
what to do in the crystalline dry? Well
below in the struts of laundry is the four-wheel-drive

vehicle in which to make an expedition
to the bush, or as we now say the Land,
the three quarters of our continent
set aside for mystic poetry.

Letters to the Winner

After the war, and just after marriage and fatherhood
ended in divorce, our neighbour won the special lottery,
an amount then equal to fifteen years of a manager's
salary at the bank, or fifty years' earnings by
a marginal farmer fermenting his clothes in the black
marinade of sweat, up in his mill-logging paddocks.

The district, used to one mailbag, now received two
every mailday. The fat one was for our neighbour.
After a dip or two, he let these bags accumulate
around the plank walls of the kitchen, over the chairs,
till on a rainy day, he fed the tail-switching calves,
let the bullocks out of the yard, and, pausing at the door
to wash his hands, came inside to read the letters.

Shaken out in a vast mound on the kitchen table
they slid down, slithered to his fingers. *I have 7 children*
I am under the doctor if you could see your way clear
equal Pardners in the Venture God would bless you lovey
assured of our best service for a mere fifteen pounds down
remember you're only lucky I knew you from the paper straightaway.

Baksheesh, hissed the pages as he flattened them, baksheesh!
mate if your interested in a fellow diggers problems
old mate a friend in need – the Great Golden Letter
having come, now he was being punished for it.
You sound like a lovely big boy we could have such times
her's my photoe Doll Im wearing my birthday swimsuit
with the right man I would share this infallible system.

When he lifted the stove's iron lid and started feeding in
the pages he'd read, they clutched and streamed up the corrugated
black chimney shaft. And yet he went on reading,
holding each page by its points, feeling an obligation
to read each crude rehearsed lie, each come-on, flat truth,
     extremity:
We might visit you the wise investor a loan a bush man like you

remember we met on Roma Street for your delight and mine
a lick of the sultana – the white moraine kept slipping
its messages to him *you will be accursed* he husked them like cobs
Mr Nouveau Jack old man my legs are all paralysed up.
Black smuts swirled weightless in the room *some good kind person*
like the nausea of a novice free-falling in a deep mine's cage
now I have lost his pension and formed a sticky nimbus round him

but he read on, fascinated by a further human range
not even war had taught him, nor literature glossed for him
since he never read literature. Merely the great reject pile
which high style is there to snub and filter, for readers.
That his one day's reading had a strong taste of what he and war
had made of his marriage is likely; he was not without sympathy,

but his leap had hit a wire through which the human is policed.
His head throbbed as if busting with a soundless shout
of immemorial sobbed invective *God-forsaken, Godforsakin*
as he stopped reading, and sat blackened in his riches.

The Milk Lorry

Now the milk lorry is a polished submarine
that rolls up at midday, attaches a trunk and inhales
the dairy's tank to a frosty snore in minutes

but its forerunner was the high-tyred barn of crisp mornings,
reeking diesel and mammary, hazy in its roped interior
as a carpet under beaters, as it crashed along potholed lanes

cooeeing at schoolgirls. Long planks like unshipped oars
butted, levelling in there, because between each farm's
stranded wharf of milk cans, the work was feverish slotting

of floors above floors, for load. It was sling out the bashed
paint-collared empties and waltz in the full,
stumbling on their rims under ribaldry, tilting their big gallons

then the schoolboy's calisthenic, hoisting steel men man-high
till the glancing hold was a magazine of casque armour,
a tinplate 'tween-decks, a seminar engrossed

in one swaying tradition, behind the speeding doorways
that tempted a truant to brace and drop, short of town,
and spend the day, with book or not, down under

the bridge of a river that by dinnertime would be
tongueing like cattledogs, or down a moth-dusty reach
where the fish-feeding milk boat and cedar barge once floated.

The Butter Factory

It was built of things that must not mix:
paint, cream and water, fire and dusty oil.
You heard the water dreaming in its large
kneed pipes, up from the weir. And the cordwood
our fathers cut for the furnace stood in walls
like the sleeper-stacks of a continental railway.

The cream arrived in lorried tides; its procession
crossed a platform of workers' stagecraft: *Come here
Friday-Legs! Or I'll feel your hernia —*
Overalled in milk's colour, men moved the heart of milk,
separated into thousands, along a roller track — *Trucks?
That one of mine, son, it pulls like a sixteen-year-old —*
to the tester who broached the can lids, causing fat tears,
who tasted, dipped and did his thin stoppered chemistry
on our labour, as the empties chattered downstage and fumed.

Under the high roof, black-crusted and stainless steels
were walled apart: black romped with leather belts
but paddlewheels sailed the silvery vats where muscles
of the one deep cream were exercised to a bullion
to be blocked in paper. And between waves of delivery
the men trod on water, hosing the rainbows of a shift.

It was damp April even at Christmas round every
margin of the factory. Also it opened the mouth
to see tackles on glibbed gravel, and the mossed char louvres
of the ice-plant's timber tower streaming with
heavy rain all day, above the droughty paddocks
of the totem cows round whom our lives were dancing.

Roman Cage-cups

Polish, at a constant curving interval, within
a layer of air between the inner and outer
skins of a glass beaker, leaving only odd struts integral.

Pause, and at the same ablative atom-
by-atom rate, sculpt the outer shell to an openwork
of rings, or foliage, or a muscular Elysium —

It made for calm paste and a steady file
that one false stroke, one twitch could cost a year's time,
a good billet, your concubine. Only the cups were held noble.

Plebs and immigrants fashioned them, punters
who ate tavern-fried pike and talked Vulgate.
The very first might have been made as a stunt, as

the life-gambit of a slave. Or a joke on the feasting scene:
a wine-bowl no one coarsely drunk could handle
nor, since baseless, easily put down,

a marvel of undercutting, a glass vessel
so costly it would exact that Roman gravity,
draw blood, and feud, if grasped without suavity.

The one depicting Thracian Lycurgus
strangled by amorous vines for slighting Bacchus
could hardly have survived an old-time bacchanal.

The glass flowers of Harvard, monks' micro pen-lace, a
    chromosome
needled to grow wings on a horse (which they'd also have done),
the freely moving ivory dragons-inside-a-dragon

ball of Cathay — the impossible is a groove:
why else do we do it? Even some given a choice
would rather work the metaphors than live them, in society.

But nothing, since sparkle became permanent in the thumbs
and rib-cages of these craftsmen, has matched their handiwork
for gentleness, or edge. They put the gape into agapé,

these factory products, of all Rome's underground Gothic:
cups transfigured by hand, too delicate to break.
Some, exported beyond the Rhine as a *miss-*

ion civilisatrice, have survived complete and unchipped
a sesquimillennium longer than the trumpets (allude,
allude) of the arena. Rome's very hardest rock.

The Lake Surnames

There are rental houseboats down the lakes now.
Two people facing, with drinks, in a restaurant party
talk about them: *That idiot, he ran us aground*
in the dark! These fishermen rescued us,
towed us off the mudbank. They were frightening actually,
real inbred faces, Deliverance people
when we saw them by torchlight in their boat —

For an instant, rain rattles at the glass
and brown cardboards of a kitchen window
and drips lamplight-coloured out of soot
in the fireplace, hitching steam off stove-iron.

Tins of beeswax, nails and poultice mixture
stick to shelves behind the door. Triangular
too, the caramel dark up under rafters
is shared, above one plank wall, by the room

where the English housekeeper screamed
at a crisp bat on the lino. Guest room,
parents' room, always called *the room*
with tennis racquet and rifle in the lowboy.

Quick steps jingle the glassed cabinet
as a figure fishes spoons from scalding water
('what's not clean's sterilised') in the board-railed
double triangle of a kerosene-tin sink,

a real Bogan sink, on the table.
The upright wireless, having died when valves vanished,
has its back to the wall. It is a *plant* for money
guarded by a nesting snake, who'll be killed when discovered.

The new car outside, streaming cricket scores,
is a sit-in radio, glowing, tightly furnished
but in the Auburn wood stove, the fire laps
and is luxury too, in one of them flood years.

– With only the briefest pause, the other
answers: *There aren't that many full-time*
surnames down the lakes. If you'd addressed them
as Mr Blanche, Mr Woodward, Mr Legge,
Mr Bramble, or Palmer, your own surname,
you'd probably have been right. And more at ease.

Nocturne

Brisbane, night-gathered, far away
estuarine imaginary city
of houses towering down one side
of slatted lights seen under leaves

confluence of ranginess with lush,
Brisbane, of rotogravure memory
approached by web lines of coke and grit
by sleepers racked in corridor trains

weatherboard incantatory city
of the timber duchess, the strapped port
in Auchenflower and Fortitude Valley
and bottletops spat in Vulture Street

greatest of the floodtime towns
that choked the dictionary with silt
and hung a navy in the tropic gardens.
Brisbane, on the steep green slope to war

brothel-humid headquarters city
where commandos and their allies fought
down café stairs, belt buckle and boot
and once with a rattletrap green gun.

In midnight nets, in mango bombings
Brisbane, storied and cable-fixed,
above your rum river, farewell and adieu
in marble on the hill of Toowong

by golfing pockets, by deep squared pockets
night heals the bubbled tar of day
and the crab moon, rising, reddens above
Brisbane, rotating far away.

Lotus Dam

Lotus leaves, standing feet above the water,
collect at their centre a perfect lens of rain
and heel, and tip it back into the water.

Their baby leaves are feet again, or slant lips
scrolled in declaration; pointed at toe and heel
they echo an unwalked sole in their pale green crinkles

and under blown and picket blooms, the floor
of floating leaves rolls light rainwater marbles
back and forth on sharkskins of anchored rippling.

Each speculum, pearl and pebble of the first water
rides, sprung with weight, on its live mirroring skin
tipped green and loganberry, till one or other sky

redeems it, beneath bent foils and ferruled canes
where cupped pink bursts all day, above riddled water.

Hearing Impairment

Hearing loss? Yes, loss is what we hear
who are starting to go deaf. Loss
trails a lot of weird puns in its wake, viz.
Dad's a real prism of the Left —
you'd like me to repeat that?
THE SAD SURREALISM OF THE DEAF.

It's mind over mutter at work
guessing half what the munglers are saying
and society's worse. Punchlines elude to you
as Henry Lawson and other touchy drinkers
have claimed. Asides, too, go pasture.
It's particularly nasty with a wether.

First you crane at people, face them
while you can still face them. But grudgually
you give up dinnier parties; you begin
to think about Beethoven; you Hanover
next visit here on silly Narda Fearing — I SAY
YOU CAN HAVE AN EXQUISITE EAR
AND STILL BE HARD OF HEARING.

It seems to be mainly speech, at first,
that escapes you – and that can be a rest,
the poor man's escape itch from Babel.
You can still hear a duck way upriver,
a lorry miles off on the highway. You
can still say boo to a goose and
read its curt yellow-lipped reply.
You can shout SING UP to a magpie,

but one day soon you must feel
the silent stopwatch chill your ear
in the doctor's rooms, and be wired
back into a slightly thinned world
with a faint plastic undertone to it
and, if the rumours are true, snatches
of static, music, police transmissions:
it's a BARF minor Car Fourteen prospect.

But maybe hearing aids are now perfect
and maybe it's not all that soon.
Sweet nothings in your ear are still sweet;
you've heard the human range by your age
and can follow most talk from memory;
the peace of the graveyard's well up
on that of the grave. And the world would
enjoy peace and birdsong for more moments

if you were head of government, enquiring
of an aide Why, Simpkins, do you tell me
a warrior is a ready flirt?
I might argue – and flowers keep blooming
as he swallows his larynx to shriek
our common mind-overloading sentence:
I'M SORRY, SIR, IT'S A RED ALERT!

At Thunderbolt's Grave in Uralla

The New England Highway was formed
by Christian men who reckoned
Adam and Eve should have been
sodomized for the curse of work
they brought on humankind,
not drudgery, but work.
No luxury of distinctions.

Those workers never went to Bali. Some set out.
But roads were game reserves to Thunderbolt
when a bridge was a leap, and wheels
were laborious, trundling through the splashways.
There were two heights of people: equestrians
and those foreshortened on foot.
All were more dressed, because more naked.

That German brass band that Thunderbolt,
attended by a pregnant boy,
bailed up on Goonoo Goonoo Gap:
'Gentlemen, if you are that poor
I'll refund your twenty pound, provided
a horse I mean to shake wins at Tenterfield.'
And it did, arching its neck, and he did
by postal note at Warwick.
Hoch! Public relations by trombone!

What woman wouldn't camp out, and wear trousers
for a man pinched and bearded as the nine
lions on the courthouse coat of arms
with their tongues saying languish and lavish,
who took her from men who gasped romance
into her lungs and offered sixpence,
from her own heart-gelded tribesfolk
and white women's dreadful eyes?

Though Uralla creek is floored with planks now
the amethystine light of New England

still seems augmented from beneath
both horizons; tin outside chimneys
still squeeze woodsmoke into the air
but the police cars come wailing their
unerotic In-Out In-Out,
red-shifting over Goonoo Goonoo.

Of all the known bushrangers,
those cropped in the floggers' gulag,
those jostled by its Crown guards,
the bolters and the hoods were merely shot
or ironed or hanged. Only three required
frenzied extermination, with rituals:
Jackey Westaway, made monstrous by torture,
Fred Ward shot and head-pulped, Ben Hall
shot dead, and for several minutes afterwards.

All three were thieves. They likely never met.
All three stole the Crown's magic pallium
and trailed it through the bush, a drag
for raging pursuit. On every snag
they left some white or blue – the red part
they threw away at once, disdaining murder.
The part they died hard for was the part
they wouldn't play, not believing the game worth murder.

Criminal noncomplicity! It was something nameless
above all stations, that critical magic
haloed in laughter. *Tell Fred I need to be robbed Friday
or I'm jiggered!* A deadly style suddenly felt lumbering,
battered with a slapstick. Our only indigenous revolution.
It took Ned Kelly to reassure policemen.

Why don't we kill like Americans?
We started to. The police were pushing it
but we weren't a republic for bringing things to a head
and these, even dying – *Are you a married man?*
cried Ward, and fired wide – helped wrong-foot mortal drama
and leave it decrepit, a police atmosphere.
In a few years, the game was boss and union.

You were a cross swell, Fred. You alone hated
to use a gang. Those always kill, as Hall learned.
I hope your children found your cache
and did good with it. They left some on deposit.

Poetry and Religion

Religions are poems. They concert
our daylight and dreaming mind, our
emotions, instinct, breath and native gesture

into the only whole thinking: poetry.
Nothing's said till it's dreamed out in words
and nothing's true that figures in words only.

A poem, compared with an arrayed religion,
may be like a soldier's one short marriage night
to die and live by. But that is a small religion.

Full religion is the large poem in loving repetition;
like any poem, it must be inexhaustible and complete
with turns where we ask Now why did the poet do that?

You can't pray a lie, said Huckleberry Finn;
you can't poe one either. It is the same mirror:
mobile, glancing, we call it poetry,

fixed centrally, we call it a religion,
and God is the poetry caught in any religion,
caught, not imprisoned. Caught as in a mirror

that he attracted, being in the world as poetry
is in the poem, a law against its closure.
There'll always be religion around while there is poetry

or a lack of it. Both are given, and intermittent,
as the action of those birds – crested pigeon, rosella parrot –
who fly with wings shut, then beating, and again shut.

May: When Bounty Is Down to Persimmons and Lemons

In May, Mary's month,
when snakes go to sleep,
sun rays and shade lengthen,
forest grows deep,

wood coughs at the axe
and splinters hurt worse,
barbed wire pulls through
every post in reverse,

old horses grow shaggy
and flies hunker down
on curtains, like sequins
on a dead girl's ball gown.

Grey soldier-birds arrive
in flickers of speed
to hang upside down
from a quivering weed

or tremble trees' foliage
that they trickle down through.
Women's Weekly summer fashions
in the compost turn blue.

The sun slants in under things
and stares right through houses;
soon pyjamas will peep, though,
from the bottoms of trousers.

Night-barking dogs quieten
as overcast forms
and it rains, with far thunder,
in queer predawn storms;

then the school bus tops ridges
with clay marks for effort,
picking up drowsy schoolkids,
none of them now barefoot,

and farmers take spanners
to the balers, gang ploughs
and towering diesel tractors
they prefer to their cows.

June: The Kitchens

This deep in the year, in the frosts of then
that steeled sheets left ghostly on the stayed line,
smoked over verandah beds, cruelled water taps rigid,
family and visitors would sit beside the lake
of blinding coals, that end of the detached kitchen,
the older fellows quoting qoph and resh
from the Book of Psalms, as they sizzled phlegm
(some still did it after iron stoves came
and the young moved off to cards and the radio)
and all told stories. That's a kind of spoken video:

We rode through from the Myall
on that road of the cedarcutter's ghost.
All this was called Wild Horses Creek then;
you could plait the grass over the pommel
of your saddle. That grass don't grow now.
I remember we camped on Waterloo that night
there where the black men gave the troopers a hiding.

The garden was all she had: the parrots were at it
and she came out and said to them, quite serious
like as if to reasonable people They are *my* peas.
And do you know? They flew off and never come back.

If you missed anything: plough,
saddle, cornplanter, shovel,
you just went across to Uncle Bob's
and brought it home. If he
was there, he never looked ashamed:
he'd just tell you a joke,
some lies, sing you a poem,
keep you there drinking all night –

Bloody cruel mongrels, telling me the native bear
would grow a new hide if you skun it alive.
Everybody knows that, they told me. I told them
if I caught any man skinning bears alive
on my place, he'd bloody need a new hide himself.

Tommy Turpin the blackfellow said to me More better
you walk behind me today, eh boss.
Might be devil-devil tell me hit you with the axe
longa back of the head. I thought he was joking
then I saw he wasn't. My word I stayed behind
that day, with the axe, trimming tongues on the rails
while he cut mortises out of the posts. I listened.

I wis eight year old, an Faither gied me the lang gun
tae gang doon an shuit the native hens at wis aitin
aa oor oats. I reasoned gin ye pit ae chairge
i the gun, pouder waddin an shot, ye got ae shot
sae pit in twa, ye'd get twa. Aweel, I pit in seven,
liggd doon ahint a stump, pu'd the trigger – an the warld
gaed milky white. I think I visited Scotland
whaur I had never been. It was a ferlie I wis seean.
It wis a sonsy place. But Grannie gard me gang back.
Mither wis skailan watter on ma heid, greetin. Aa they found
o the gun wis stump-flinders, but there wis a black scour thro the
    oats,
an unco ringan in ma ears, an fifteen deid native hens.

Of course long tongue she laughed about that other
and they pumped her about you can guess and
hanging round there
and she said He's got one on him like a horse, Mama,
and I like it. Well! And all because of you know –

Father couldn't stand meanness.
When Uncle you-know-who
charged money for milking our cows
that time Isabel took bad
Father called him gutless,
not just tin-arsed, but gutless.
Meanness is for cowards, Father reckoned.

The little devil, he says to the minister's wife
Daddy reckons we can't have any more children,
we need the milk for the pigs. Dear I was mortified –

Poor Auntie Mary was dying Old and frail
all scroopered down in the bedclothes pale as cotton
even her hardworking old hands Oh it was sad
people in the room her big daughters performing
rattling the bedknobs There is a white angel
in the room says Mary in this weird voice And then
NO! she heaves herself up Bloody no! Be quiet!
she coughed and spat Phoo! I'll be damned if I'll die!
She's back making bread next week Lived ten more years.

Well, it was black Navy rum; it buggered Darcy.
Fell off his horse, crawled under the cemetery fence.
Then some yahoos cantered past Yez all asleep in there?
All but me, croaks Darcy. They off at a hand gallop,
squealing out, and his horse behind them, stirrups belting it.

The worst ghost I ever saw
was a policeman and (one of the squatters)
moving cattle at night.
I caught them in my headlights.
It haunted me. Every time
I went in to town after that
somehow I'd get arrested –

I'll swear snakes have got no brains!
The carpet snake we had in the rafters
to eat rats, one day it et a chook.
I killed it with the pitchfork, ran a tine
through the top of its head, and chucked it
down the gully. It was back in a week
with a scab on its head and another under its chin.
They bring a house good luck but they got no brain.

Then someone might cup his hand short of the tongue
of a taut violin, try each string to be wrung
by the bow, that spanned razor of holy white hair
and launch all but his earthly weight into an air
that breathed up hearth fires strung worldwide between
the rung hills of being and the pearled hills of been.
In the language beyond speaking they'd sum the grim law,
speed it to a daedaly and foot it to a draw,
the tones of their scale five gnarled fingers wide
and what sang were all angles between love and pride.

July: Midwinter Haircut

Now the world has stopped. Dead middle of the year.
Cloud all the colours of a worn-out dairy bucket
freeze-frames the whole sky. The only sun is down
intensely deep in the dam's bewhiskered mirror
and the white-faced heron hides in the drain with her spear.

Now the world has stopped, doors could be left open.
Only one fly came awake to the kitchen heater
this breakfast time, and supped on a rice bubble sluggishly.
No more will come inside out of the frost-crimped grass now.
Crime, too, sits in faraway cars. Phone lines drop at the
    horizon.

Now the world has stopped, what do we feel like doing?
The district's former haircutter, from the time before barbers, has shaved
and wants a haircut. So do I. No longer the munching hand clippers
with locks in their gears, nor the scissors more pointed than a beak
but the buzzing electric clipper, straight from its cardboard giftbox.

We'll sit under that on the broad-bottomed stool that was
the seat for fifty years of the district's only sit-down job,
the postmistress-telephonist's seat, where our poor great-aunt
who trundled and spoke in sour verdicts sat to hand-crank
the tingling exchange, plugged us into each other's lives

and tapped consolation from gossip's cells as they unlidded.
From her shrewd kind successor who never tapped in, and planes
along below the eaves of our heads, we'll hear a tapestry
of weddings funerals surgeries, and after our sittings
be given a jar of pickle. Hers won't be like the house

a mile down the creek, where cards are cut and shuffled
in the middle of the day, and mortarbombs of beer
detonate the digestion, and they tell world-stopping yarns
like: I went to Sydney races. There along the rails, all snap brims
        and cold eyes, flanked by senior police

    and other, stony men with their eyes in a single crease
    stood the entire Government of New South Wales
    watching Darby ply the whip, all for show, over this fast colt.
    It was young and naïve. It was heading for the post in a bolt
    while the filly carrying his and all the inside money

    strained to come level. Too quick for the stewards to note him
    Darby slipped the colt a low lash to the scrotum.
    It checked, shocked, stumbled – and the filly flashed by.
    As he came from weighing in, I caught Darby's eye
    and he said *Get out of it, mug,* quite conversationally –

August: Forty Acre Ethno

The Easter rains are late this year
at this other end of a dry hard winter.
Low clouds grow great rustling crops of fall
and all the gully-courses braid and bubble,
their root-braced jugs and coarse lips pour
and it's black slog for cows when, grass lake to puddle,
a galloping dog sparks on all four.
It'll be plashy England here for a while
or boggy Scotland, by the bent straw colour
and the breaks of sun mirror-backed with chill.

Coming home? It was right. And it was time.
I had been twenty-nine years away
after books and work and society
but society vanished into ideology
and by then I could bring the other two home.
We haven't been out at night since we came
back, except last month, in the United Kingdom.
The towns ranged like footlights up the highway
and coastline here rehearse a subtle play
that's only staged in private by each family.

Sight and life restored by an eye operation
my father sits nightly before the glass screen
of a wood-burning slow combustion stove. We see
the same show, with words, on television.
Dad speaks of memories, and calls his fire homely:
when did you last hear that word without scorn
for something unglossy, or some poor woman?
Here, where thin is *poor*, and fat is *condition*,
'homely' is praise and warmth, spoken gratefully.
Its opposite lurks outside in dark blowing rain.

Horses are exposed to it, wanly stamping out
unglazed birth ware for mosquitoes in the coming season
and already peach trees are a bare wet frame
for notional little girls in pink dots of gingham.

Cars coming home fishtail and harrow the last mile,
their undersea headlights kicking gum trees around eerily;
woodducks wake high in those trees, and peer from the door
they'll shove their ducklings out of, to spin down in their down,
sprawl, and swim to water. Our children dog the footsteps
of their grandfather, learning their ancient culture.

September: Mercurial

Preindustrial haze. The white sky rim
forecasts a hot summer. Burning days
indeed are rehearsed, with flies and dinnertime fan,
but die out, over west mountains
erased with azure, into spring-cool nights
and the first flying insects
which are the small weeds of a bedroom window.

Early in the month, the valley was a Friesian cow:
knobbed black, whitened straw.
Alarming smokes bellied up behind the heights of forest.
Now green has invested fires'
fixed cloud-shadows; lower gum boughs are seared chestnut.
Emerald kingparrots, crimson-breasted, whirr
and plane out of open feed sheds.

Winds are changeable. We're tacking.
West on rubbed blue days,
easterlies on hot, southerly and dead calm for rain.
Mercury is near the moon, Venus at perigee
and frogs wind their watches all night on swampy stretches
where waterhens blink with their tails at dusk, like rabbits
and the mother duck does her cripple act.

Dams glitter like house roofs again.
The first wasp comes looking for a spider to paralyse:
a flimsy ultralight flier
who looks like a pushover, but after one pass lifts

you, numb, out of your trampoline. Leaves together
as for prayer or diving, bean plants erupt
into the grazing glory. Those unnibbled spread their arms.

Poddy calves wobbling in their newborn mushroom colours
ingest and make the pungent custard of infancy.
Sign of a good year, many snakes lie flattened
on the roads again. Bees and pollens drift
through greening orchards. And next day it pours rain:
smokes of cloud on every bushland slope,
that opposite, wintry haze. The month goes out facing backwards.

November: The Misery Cord

in memory of F.S. Murray

Misericord. The Misery Cord.
It was lettered on a wall.
I knew that cord, how it's tough to break
however hard you haul.

My cousin sharefarmed, and so got half:
half dignity, half hope, half income,
for his full work. To get a place
of his own took his whole lifetime.

Some pluck the misery chord from habit
or for luck, however they feel,
some to deceive, and some for the tune –
but sometimes it's real.

Milking bails, flannel shirts, fried breakfasts,
these were our element,
and doubling on horses, and shouting Score!
at a dog yelping on a hot scent –

but an ambulance racing on our back road
is bad news for us all:
the house of community is about
to lose a plank from its wall.

Grief is nothing you can do, but do,
worst work for least reward,
pulling your heart out through your eyes
with tugs of the misery cord.

I looked at my cousin's farm, where he'd just
built his family a house of their own,
and I looked down into Fred's next house,
its clay walls of bluish maroon.

Just one man has broken the misery cord
and lived. He said once was enough.
A poem is an afterlife on earth:
Christ grant us the other half.

December: Infant Among Cattle

Young parents, up at dawn, working. Their first child can't
be his own babysitter, so as they machine the orphaned milk
from their cows, he must sit plump on the dairy cement,
the back of his keyhole pants safetypinned to a stocking

that is tied to a bench leg. He studies a splotch of cream,
how the bubbles in it, too thick to break, work like
the coated and lucid gravels in the floor. On which he then dings
a steel thing, for the tingling in it and his fingers

till it skips beyond his tether. As the milkers front up
in their heel-less skiddy shoes, he hangs out aslant
on his static line, watching the breeching rope brace them
and their washed udders relieved of the bloodberry ticks

that pull off a stain, and show a calyx of kicking filaments.
By now the light stands up behind the trees like sheet iron.
It photographs the cowyard and dairy-and-bails in one vast
buttery shadow wheel on the trampled junction of paddocks

where the soil is itself a concrete, of dust and seedy stones
and manure crustings. When his father slings a bucketful
of wash water out the door, it wallops and skids
and is gulped down by a sudden maw like the cloth of a radio.

Out and on out, the earth tightens down on the earth
and squeezes heat up through the yellow grass
like a surfaceless fluid, to pool on open country,
to drip from faces, and breed the insect gleams of midday.

Under the bench, crooning this without words to his rag dog,
he hears a vague trotting outside increase − and the bull
erupts, aghast, through the doorway, dribbling, clay in his curls,
a slit orange tongue working in and out under his belly −

and is repulsed, with buckets and screams and a shovel.
The little boy, swept up in his parents' distress, howls then
but not in fear of the bull, who seemed a sad apparition:
a huge prostrate man, bewildered by a pitiless urgency.

February: Feb

Seedy drytime Feb,
lightning between its teeth,
all its plants pot-bound.

Inside enamelled rims
dams shrink their mirroring shields,
baking the waterlilies.

Days stacked like clay pigeons
squeezed from dust and sweat.
Two cultures: sun and shade.

Days dazed with actuality
like a bottle shot
sniping fruit off twigs,

by afternoon, portentous
with whole cloud–Atlantics
that rain fifteen drops.

Beetroot and iron butter,
bread staled by the fan,
cold chook: that's lunch with Feb.

Weedy drymouth Feb, first cousin of scorched creek stones,
of barbed wire across gaunt gullies, bringer of soldered
death-freckles to the backs of farmers' hands. The mite-struck

foal rattles her itch on fence wires, like her mother,
and scraped hill pastures are grazed back to their charred
bulldozer stitchings. Dogs nip themselves under the tractor

of needy Feb, who waits for the raw eel-perfume
of the first real rain's pheromones, the magic rain-on-dust
sexual scent of Time itself, philtre of all native beings –

Lanky cornhusk Feb,
drilling the red-faced
battalions of tomatoes

through the grader's slots:
harvest out of bareness,
that semidesert mode.

Worn grasshopper month
suddenly void of children;
days tucking their tips in

with blackberry seeds to spit
and all of life root-bound;
stringy dryland Feb.

The Transposition of Clermont

After the Big Flood, we elected
to move our small timber city
from the dangerous beauty of the river
and its fringed lagoons
since both had risen to destroy us.

Many buildings went stacked on wagons
but more were towed entire
in strained stateliness, with a long groyning sound,
up timber by traction engines.

Each moved singly. Life went on round them;
in them, at points of rest.
Guests at breakfast in the Royal Hotel, facing
now the saddlery, now the Town Hall.

We drank in the canted Freemasons
and the progressive Shamrock, but really
all pubs were the Exchange. Relativities
interchanged our world like a chess game:

butcher occluded baker, the police
eclipsed both brothels, the dance hall
sashayed around the Temperance Hall,
front doors sniffed rear, and thoughtfully ground on.

Certain houses burst, and vanished.
One wept its windows, one trailed mementoes up the street.
A taut chain suddenly parted and scythed down
horses and a verandah. Weed-edged black rectangles
in exploded gardens yielded sovereigns and spoons.

That ascent of working architecture
onto the pegged plateau was a children's crusade
with lines stretching down to us.
Everything standing in its wrong accustomed place.
My generation's memories are intricately transposed:

97

butcher occluding dance music, the police
eclipsed by opportunity, brothels sashaying royally
and, riding sidesaddle up shined skids, the Town Hall.
Excited, we would meet on streets that stayed immutable

sometimes for weeks; from irrecoverable corners
and alleys already widening, we'd look
back down at our new graves and childhood gardens,
the odd house at anchor for a quick tomato season
and the swaying nailed hull of a church going on before us.

And many allotments left unbought, or for expansion
never filled up, above, as they hadn't below.
What was town, what was country stayed elusive
as we saw it always does, in the bush,
what is waste, what is space, what is land.

Cave Divers Near Mount Gambier

Chenille-skinned people are counting under the countryside
on resurrections by truck light off among the pines.

Here in the first paddocks, where winter comes ashore,
mild duckweed ponds are skylights of a filled kingdom

and what their gaze absorbs may float up districts away.
White men with scorches of hair approach that water,

zip into black, upturn large flap feet and free-fall
away, their mouths crammed full. Crystalline polyps

of their breathing blossom for a while, as they disturb
algal screens, extinct kangaroos, eels of liquorice colour

then, with the portable greening stars they carry under,
these vanish, as the divers undergo tight anti-births

into the vaults and profound domes of the limestone.
Here, approaching the heart of the poem they embody

and thereby make the gliding cavern-world embody,
they have to keep time with themselves, and be dull often

with its daylight logic – since to dream it fully
might leave them asprawl on the void clang of their tanks,

their faceplates glazing an unfocused dreadful portrait
at the apex of a steeple that does not reach the day.

The Tin Wash Dish

Lank poverty, dank poverty,
its pants wear through at fork and knee.
It warms its hands over burning shames,
refers to its fate as Them and He
and delights in things by their hard names:
rag and toejam, feed and paw –
don't guts that down, there ain't no more!
Dank poverty, rank poverty,
it hums with a grim fidelity
like wood-rot with a hint of orifice,
wet newspaper jammed in the gaps of artifice,
and disgusts us into fierce loyalty.
It's never the fault of those you love:
poverty comes down from above.
Let it dance chairs and smash the door,
it arises from all that went before
and every outsider's the enemy –
Jesus Christ turned this over with his stick
and knights and philosophers turned it back.
Rank poverty, lank poverty,
chafe in its crotch and sores in its hair,
still a window's clean if it's made of air,
not webby silver like a sleeve.

Watch out if this does well at school
and has to leave and longs to leave:
someone, sometime, will have to pay.
Shave with toilet soap, run to flesh,
astound the nation, rule the army,
still you wait for the day you'll be sent back
where books or toys on the floor are rubbish
and no one's allowed to come and play
because home calls itself a shack
and hot water crinkles in the tin wash dish.

The Inverse Transports

Two hundred years, and the bars
reappear on more and more windows;
more people have a special number to ring.
This started with furious strange Christians:
they would have all things in common,
have morals superseded by love —
truth and Christ they rejected scornfully.

More people sell and move to the country.
The bush becomes their civil city.
What do they do there? Some make quilts
sewing worn and washed banknotes together.
What romantic legends do they hear there?
Tales of lineage, and of terrible accidents:
the rearing tractor, the sawmills' bloody moons.

Accident is the tiger of the country,
but fairytale is a reserve, for those rich only
in that and fifty thousand years here.
The incomers will acquire those fifty thousand
years too, though. Thousands of anything
draw them. They discovered thousands,
even these. Which they offer now, for settlement.

Has the nation been a poem or an accident?
And which should it be? America, and the Soviets
and the First and Third Reich were poems.
Two others, quite different, have been Rome's.
We've been through some bloody British stanzas
and some local stanzas where 'pelf'
was the rhyme for 'self' – and some about police,

refuge, ballots, space, the Fair Go and peace.
Many strain now to compose a National Purpose,
some fear its enforcement. Free people take liberties:
inspired government takes liberty itself.
Takes it where, court to parliament to bureaucracy
to big union to gaol, an agreed atmosphere
endures, that's dealt with God and democracy.

Inside convict ships that Christ's grace inverted
hanging chains end in lights. Congregations
approach the classless there. But the ships are being buried
in tipped dirt. Half the media denies
it's happening, and the other half justifies
this live burial – and the worshippers divide likewise
in their views of the sliding waves of garbage

in which their ships welter and rise
beneath towers with the lyric sheen of heroin
that reach skyward out of the paradox
that expression and achievement are the Prize
and at the same time are indefensible privilege.
Two hundred years, and the bars
appear on more and more windows.

The Pole Barns

Unchinked log cabins, empty now, or stuffed with hay
under later iron. Or else roofless, bare stanzas of timber
with chars in the text. Each line ends in memorial axemanship.

With a hatch in one gable end, like a cuckoo clock,
they had to be climbed up into, or swung into
from the saddle of a quiet horse, feet-first onto corn.

On logs like rollers these rooms stand on creek flat and ridge,
and their true roofs were bark, every squared sheet a darkened
huge stroke of painting, fibrous from the brush.

Flattened, the sheets strained for a long time to curl again:
the man who slept on one and woke immobilised
in a scroll pipe is a primal pole-barn story.

The sound of rain on bark roofing, dotted, not pointed,
increasing to a sonic blanket, is millennia older than walls
but it was still a heart of storytelling, under the one lantern

as the comets of corn were stripped to their white teeth
and chucked over the partition, and the vellum husks shuffled
    down
round spooky tellers hunched in the planes of winter wind.

More a daylight thinker was the settler who noticed the tide
of his grain going out too fast, and set a dingo trap
in the servery slot — and found his white-faced neighbour,

a man bearded as himself, up to the shoulder in anguish.
Neither spoke as the trap was released, nor mentioned that dawn
    ever.
Happiest, in that iron age, were sitting aloft on the transom

unscrewing corn from cobs, making a good shower for the hens
and sailing the barn, with its log ram jutting low in front.
Like all the ships of conquest, its name was Supply.

Glaze

Tiles are mostly abstract:
tiles come from Islam:
tiles have been through fire:
tiles are a sacred charm:

After the unbearable parallel
trajectories of lit blank tile,
figure-tiles restore the plural,
figuring resumes its true vein.

Harm fades from the spirit as tiles
repeat time beyond time their riddle,
neat stanzas that rhyme from the middle
styles with florets with tendrils of balm.

Henna and mulberry mosaics
controvert space:
lattice on lattice recedes
through itself into Paradise

or parrot starbursts framing themes
of stars bursting, until they salaam
the Holy Name in sprigged consonants
crosslaced as Welsh metrical schemes.

Conjunct, the infinite doorways
of the mansions of mansions amaze
underfoot in a cool court, with sun-blaze
afloat on the hard water of glaze.

Ur shapes under old liquor
ziggurats of endless incline;
cruciform on maiolica
flourishes the true vine.

Tulip tiles on the grate of Humoresque
Villa join, by a great arabesque
cream boudoirs of Vienna, then by left-
handed rhyme, the blue pubs of Delft

and prominence stands in a circle
falling to the centre of climb:
O miming is defeated by mime:
circles circle the PR of ominence.

Cool Mesach in fused Rorschach,
old from beyond Islam,
tiles have been to Paradise,
clinkers of ghostly calm.

Shale Country

Watermelon rinds around the house,
small gondolas of curling green
lined with sodden rosy plush;
concrete paths edged with kerosene,

tricycles and shovels in the yard
where the septic tank makes a fairy ring;
a wire gate leads into standing wheat,
cream weatherboard overlaps everything –

and on the wheatless side, storm-blue
plaques curl off the spotted-gum trees
which, in new mayonnaise trunks, stand over
a wheelbarrow on its hands and knees.

The International Terminal

Some comb oil, some blow air,
some shave trenchlines in their hair
but the common joint thump, the heart's spondee
kicks off in its rose-lit inner sea
like an echo, at first, of the one above
it on the dodgy ladder of love –

and my mate who's driving says *I never*
found one yet worth staying with forever.
In this our poems do not align.
Surely most are if you are, answers mine,
and I am living proof of it,
I gloom, missing you from the cornering outset –
and hearts beat mostly as if they weren't there,
rocking horse to rocking chair,
most audible dubbed on the tracks of movies
or as we approach where our special groove is
or our special fear. The autumn-vast
parking-lot-bitumen overcast
now switches on pumpkin-flower lights
all over dark green garden sites
and a wall of car-bodies, stacked by blokes,
obscures suburban signs and smokes.
Like coughs, cries, all such unlearned effects
the heartbeat has no dialects
but what this or anything may mean
depends on what poem we're living in.
Now a jet engine, huge child of a gun,
shudders with haze and begins to run.
Over Mount Fuji and the North Pole
I'm bound for Europe in a reading role
and a poem long ago that was coming for me
had Fuji-san as its axle-tree.
Cities shower and rattle over the gates
as I enter that limbo between states
but I think of the heart swarmed round by poems
like an egg besieged by chromosomes
and how out of that our world is bred
through the back of a mirror, with clouds in its head
– and airborne, with a bang, this five-hundred-seat
theatre folds up its ponderous feet.

Granite Country

Out above the level
in enormous room
beyond the diagram fences
eggs of the granite loom.

In droughts' midday hum,
at the crack of winter,
horizons of the tableland
are hatched out of them

and that levelling forces
all the more to rise
past swamp, or thumbwhorled ploughing,
tor, shellback, cranium

in unended cold eruption.
Forces and strains of granite
ascended from a kingdom
abandon over centuries

their craft on the sky-rim,
sprung and lichened hatches,
as, through gaps in silence, what
made itself granite comes home.

Dog Fox Field

The test for feeblemindedness was, they had to make up a sentence using
the words dog, fox and field. —Judgement at Nuremberg

These were no leaders, but they were first
into the dark on Dog Fox Field:

Anna who rocked her head, and Paul
who grew big and yet giggled small,

Irma who looked Chinese, and Hans
who knew his world as a fox knows a field.

Hunted with needles, exposed, unfed,
this time in their thousands they bore sad cuts

for having gaped, and shuffled, and failed
to field the lore of prey and hound

they then had to thump and cry in the vans
that ran while stopped in Dog Fox Field.

Our sentries, whose holocaust does not end,
they show us when we cross into Dog Fox Field.

Hastings River Cruise

i.m. Ruth and Harry Liston, d. Port Macquarie 1826

Getting under way in that friendly suburb of balconies
we were invited to imagine up to thirty woollen ships
and timber ships and beef ships with fattening sails
along the one-time quay. Then down Heaven-blued
olive water of the estuary, we saw how ocean's crystal
penned up riverine tinctures. On our coast, every river
is a lake, for lack of force, and lives within its colour bar.

Upstream, past the bullock-faced and windjammer-ballasted shore
we passed where men in canary flannel were worked barefoot
on oystershells in shark tides. No one's walked in Australia
since, for pride and sympathy. Sheds lay offshore, pegged to the water
and lascivious oysters, though they are nearly all tongue
didn't talk drink, on their racks of phlegm, but lived it.
Opposite lay the acre where Queensland was first planted

as the pineapple of cropped heads in hot need of sugar walls.
There too, by that defiance, were speedboat mansions up canals
and no prescriptive ulcers or divorces apparent in them
though one, built late in life perhaps, spilled grapefruit down its
    lawns.
And the river curved on, and a navy-backed elephant stood
in the mountains for mission boys who stepped right up, through
    the drum,
and belted blue eyes into red-leather Kingdom Come.

At the highway bridge, in sight of plateaux, we turned back
and since the shore of the present was revetments and raw brick
or else flood-toppled trees with mullet for foliage, I looked
over at the shore of the past. Rusty paddocks, with out-of-date
    palms,
punt ramps where De Sotos crossed; there, in houses patched
    with tan,
breezeways wound to green bedrooms with framed words like
    He Moaneth,
the sort of country I might traverse during death.

Returning downstream, over the Regatta Ground's liquid tiling,
we passed through the place where, meeting his only sister
in a new draft to the Port, the tugged escapee snatched the musket
of a redcoat captor, aimed and shot her dead –
and was saluted for it, as he strangled, by the Commandant.
In sight of new motels, this opposite potential stayed defined
and made the current town look remote, and precarious, and kind.

Words of the Glassblowers

In a tacky glass-foundry yard, that is shadowy and bright
as an old painter's sweater stiffening with light,

another lorry chockablock with bottles gets the raised thumb
and there hoists up a wave like flashbulbs feverish in a stadium

before all mass, nosedive and ditch, colour showering to grit,
starrily, mutually, becoming the crush called cullet

which is fired up again, by a thousand degrees, to a mucilage
and brings these reddened spearmen bantering on stage.

Each fishes up a blob, smoke-sallow with a tinge of beer
which begins, at a breath, to distil from weighty to clear

and, spinning, is inflated to a word: the paraison
to be marvered on iron, box-moulded, or whispered to while
  spun —

Sand, sauce-bottle, hourglass — we melt them into one thing:
that old Egyptian syrup, that tightens as we teach it to sing.

High Sugar

Honey gave sweetness
to Athens and Rome,
and later, when splendour
might rise nearer home,

sweetness was still honey
since, pious or lax,
every cloister had its apiary
for honey and wax

but when kings and new doctrines
drained those deep hives
then millions of people
were shipped from their lives

to grow the high sugar
from which were refined
frigates, perukes, human races
and the liberal mind.

On Removing Spiderweb

Like summer silk its denier
but stickily, o ickilier,
miffed bunny-blinder, silver tar,
gesticuli-gesticular,
crepe when cobbed, crap when rubbed,
stretchily adhere-and-there
and everyway, nap-snarled or sleek,
glibly hubbed with grots to tweak:
ehh weakly bobbined tae yer neb,
spit it Phuoc Tuy! filthy web!

The Assimilation of Background

Driving on that wide jute-coloured country
we came at last to the station,
its homestead with lawn and steel awnings
like a fortress against the sun.
And when we knocked, no people answered;
only a black dog came politely
and accompanied us round the verandahs
as we peered into rooms, and called brightly
Anyone home? The billiard room,
shadowed dining room, gauze-tabled kitchen
gave no answer. Cricket bats, ancient
steamer trunks, the chugging coolroom engine
disregarded us. Only the dog's very patient
claws ticked with us out of the gloom
to the grounds' muffling dust, to the machine shed
black with oil and bolts, with the welder
mantis-like on its cylinder of clocks
and then to the stallion's enclosure.

The great bay horse came up to the wire,
gold flares shifting on his muscles, and stood
as one ungelded in a thousand

of his race, but imprisoned for his sex,
a gene-transmitting engine, looking at us
gravely as a spirit, out between
his brain's potent programmes. Then a heifer,
Durham-roan, but with Brahman hump and rings
around her eyes, came and stood among us
and a dressy goat in sable and brushed fawn
ogled us for offerings beyond
the news all had swiftly gathered from us
in silence, and could, it seemed, accept.
We had been received, and no one grew impatient
but only the dog, host-like, walked with us
back to our car. The lawn-watering sprays
ticked over, and over. And we saw
that out on that bare, crusted country
background and foreground had merged;
nothing that existed there was background.

Accordion Music

A backstrapped family Bible that consoles virtue and sin,
for it opens top and bottom, and harps both out and in:

it shuffles a deep pack of cards, flirts an inverted fan
and stretches to a shelf of books about the pain of man.

It can play the sob in Jesus!, the cavernous *baastards* note,
it can wheedle you for cigarettes or drop a breathy quote:

it can conjure Paris up, or home, unclench a chinstrap jaw
but it never sang for a nob's baton, or lured the boys to war.

Underneath the lone streetlight outside a crossroads hall
where bullocks pass and dead girls waltz and mental gum trees fall

two brothers play their plough-rein days and long gone
    spoon-licked nights.
The fiddle stitching through this quilt lifts up in singing flights,

the other's mourning, meaning tune goes arching up and down
as life undulates like a heavy snake through the rocked accordion.

Ariel

Upward, cheeping, on huddling wings,
these small brown mynas have gained
a keener height than their kind ever sustained
but whichever of them fails first
falls to the hawk circling under
who drove them up.
Nothing's free when it is explained.

Politics and Art

Brutal policy,
like inferior art, knows
whose fault it all is.

The Ballad of the Barbed Wire Ocean

No more rice pudding. Pink coupons for Plume. Smokes under
    the lap for aunts.
Four running black boots beside a red sun. Flash wireless words
    like Advarnce.
When the ocean was wrapped in barbed wire, terror radiant up
    the night sky,
exhilaration raced flat out in squadrons; Mum's friends took off
    sun-hats to cry.

Starting south of the then world with new showground rifles
    being screamed at and shown
for a giggle-suit three feeds a day and no more plans of your
    own,
it went with some swagger till God bless you, Tom! and Daddy
    come back! at the train
or a hoot up the gangways for all the girls and soon the coast
    fading in rain,

but then it was flared screams from blood-bundles whipped
    rolling as iron bombs keened down
and the insect-eyed bombers burned their crews alive in off-
    register henna and brown.
In steep ruins of rainforest pre-affluent thousands ape-scuttling
    mixed sewage with blood
and fear and the poem played vodka to morals, fear jolting to the
    mouth like cud.

It was sleep atop supplies, it was pickhandle, it was coming
    against the wall in tears,
sometimes it was factory banter, stoking jerked breechblocks and
    filing souvenirs,
or miles-wide humming cattleyards of humans, or oiled ship-fires
    slanting in ice,
rag-wearers burst as by huge War Bonds coins, girls' mouths full
    of living rice.

No one came home from it. Phantoms smoked two hundred
    daily. Ghosts held civilians at bay,
since war turns beyond strut and adventure to keeping what
    you've learned, and shown,
what you've approved, and what you've done, from ever
    reaching your own.
This is died for. And nihil and nonsense feed on it day after day.

Midnight Lake

Little boy blue, four hours till dawn.
Your bed's a cement bag, your plastic is torn.

Your breakfast was tap water, dinner was sleep;
you are the faith your olds couldn't keep.

In your bunny rug room there were toys on the floor
but nothing is obvious when people get poor

and newspaper crackles next to your skin.
You're a newspaper fairytale now, Tommy Thin,

a postnatal abortion, slick outer space thing,
you run like a pinball BING! smack crack BING!

then, strung out and spotty, you wriggle and sigh
and kiss all the fellows and make them all die.

Antarctica

Beyond the human flat earths
which, policed by warm language, wreathe
in fog the limits of the world,
far out in space you can breathe

the planet revolves in a cold book.
It turns one numb white page a year.
Round this in shattering billions spread
ruins of a Ptolemaic sphere,

and brittle-beard reciters bore
out time in adamant hoar rods
to freight where it's growing short,
childless absolutes shrieking the odds.

Most modern of the Great South Lands,
her storm-blown powder whited wigs
as wit of the New Contempt chilled her.
The first spacefarers worked her rope rigs

in horizontal liftoff, when to climb
the high Pole was officer class.
Total prehuman pavement, extending
beyond every roof-brink of crevasse:

Sterility Park, ringed by sheathed animals.
Singing spiritoso their tongueless keens
musselled carollers fly under the world.
Deeper out, our star's gale folds and greens.

Blue miles above the first flowered hills
towers the true Flood, as it was,
as it is, at the crux of global lattice,
and long-shod humans, risking diamond there,
propitiate it with known laws and our wickedness.

Blue Roan

for Philip Hodgins

As usual up the Giro mountain
dozers were shifting the road about
but the big blue ranges looked permanent
and the stinging-trees held no hint of drought.

All the high drill and blanket ridges
were dusty for want of winter rains
but down in the creases of picnic oak
brown water moved like handled chains.

Steak-red Herefords, edged like steaks
with that creamy fat the health trade bars
nudged, feeding, settling who'd get horned
and who'd horn, in the Wingham abattoirs

and men who remembered droughttime grass
like three days' growth on a stark red face
described farms on the creeks, fruit trees and fun
and how they bought out each little place.

Where farm families once would come just to watch
men knock off work, on the Bulliac line,
the fear of helplessness still burned live brush.
Dirty white smoke sent up its scattered sign

and in at the races and out at home
the pump of morale was primed and bled:
'Poor Harry in the street, beer running out his eyes,'
as the cousin who married the baker said.

The Gaelic Long Tunes

On Sabbath days, on circuit days,
the Free Church assembled from boats and gigs
and between sermons they would tauten
and, exercising all they allowed of art,
haul on the long lines of the Psalms.

The seated precentor, touching text,
would start alone, lifting up his whale-long tune
and at the right quaver, the rest set sail
after him, swaying, through eerie and lorn.
No unison of breaths-in gapped their sound.

In disdain of all theatrics, they raised
straight ahead, from plank rows, their beatless God-paean,
their giving like enduring. And in rise
and undulation, in Earth-conquest mourned
as loss, all tragedy drowned, and that weird
music impelled them, singing, like solar wind.

Wagtail

Willy Wagtail
sings at night
black and white
Oz nightingale
    picks spiders off wall
    nest-fur and eyesocket
    ticks off cows
    cattle love that
Busy daylong
eating small species
makes little faeces
and a great wealth of song
    Will and Willa Wagtail
    indistinguishable
    switchers, whizzers
    drinkers out of scissors
    weave a tiny unit
    kids clemming in it
Piping in tizzes
two fight off one
even one eagle
    little gun swingers
    rivertop ringers
    one-name-for-all
    whose lives flow by heart
    beyond the liver
    into lives of a feather
Wag it here, Willy
pretty it there
flicker and whirr –
if you weren't human
how many would care?

Bats' Ultrasound

Sleeping-bagged in a duplex wing
with fleas, in rock-cleft or building
radar bats are darkness in miniature,
their whole face one tufty crinkled ear
with weak eyes, fine teeth bared to sing.

Few are vampires. None flit through the mirror.
Where they flutter at evening's a queer
tonal hunting zone above highest C.
Insect prey at the peak of our hearing
drone re to their detailing tee:

ah, eyrie-ire, aero hour, eh?
O'er our ur-area (our era aye
ere your raw row) we air our array,
err, yaw, row wry — aura our orrery,
our eerie ü our ray, our arrow.

A rare ear, our aery Yahweh.

Eagle Pair

We shell down on the sleeping-branch. All night
the limitless Up digests its meats of light.

The circle-winged Egg then emerging from long pink and brown
re-inverts life, and meats move or are still on the Down.

Irritably we unshell, into feathers; we lean open and rise
and magnify this meat, then that, with the eyes of our eyes.

Meat is light, it is power and Up, as we free it from load
and our mainstay, the cunningest hunter, is the human road

but all the Down is heavy and tangled. Only meat is good there
and the rebound heat ribbing up vertical rivers of air.

Two Dogs

Enchantment creek underbank pollen, are the stiff scents he makes,
hot grass rolling and rabbit-dig but only saliva chickweed.
Road pizza clay bird, hers answer him, rot-spiced good. Blady grass,
she adds, ant log in hot sunshine. Snake two sunups back. Orifice?
Orifice, he wriggles. Night fox? Night fox, with left pad wound.
Cement bag, hints his shoulder. Catmeat, boasts his tail, twice
      enjoyed.
Folded sapless inside me, she clenches. He retracts initial blood.
Frosty darks coming, he nuzzles. High wind rock human-free howl,
her different law. Soon. Away, away, eucalypts speeding –
Bark! I water for it. Her eyes go binocular, as in pawed
hop frog snack play. Come ploughed, she jumps, ground. Bark
      tractor,
white bitterhead grub and pull scarecrow. Me! assents his urine.

Cockspur Bush

I am lived. I am died.
I was two-leafed three times, and grazed,
but then I was stemmed and multiplied,
sharp-thorned and caned, nested and raised,
earth-salt by sun-sugar. I am innerly sung
by thrushes who need fear no eyed skin thing.
Finched, ant-run, flowered, I am given the years
in now fewer berries, now more of sling
out over directions of luscious dung.
Of water the crankshaft, of gases the gears
my shape is cattle-pruned to a crown spread sprung
above the starve-gut instinct to make prairies
of everywhere. My thorns are stuck with caries

of mice and rank lizards by the butcher bird.
Inches in, baby seed-screamers get supplied.
I am lived and died in, vine-woven, multiplied.

Lyrebird

Liar made of leaf-litter, quivering ribby in shim,
hen-sized under froufrou, chinks in a quiff display him
or her, dancing in mating time, or out. And in any order.
Tailed mimic aeon-sent to intrigue the next recorder,
I mew catbird, I saw crosscut, I howl she-dingo, I kink
forest hush distinct with bellbirds, warble magpie garble, link
cattlebell with kettle-boil; I rank ducks' cranky presidium
or simulate a triller like a rill mirrored lyrical to a rim.
I ring dim. I alter nothing. Real to real only I sing,
Gahn the crane to Gun the chainsaw, urban thing to being,
Screaming woman owl and human talk: eedieAi and uddyunnunoan.
The miming is all of I. Silent, they are a function
of wet forest, cometary lyrebirds. Their flight lifts them barely a
    semitone.

Shoal

Eye-and-eye eye an eye
each. What blinks is I,
unison of the whole shoal. Thinks:
a dark idea circling by –
again the eyes' I winks.
Eye-and-eye near no eye
is no I, though gill-pulse drinks
and nervy fins spacewalk. Jinx
jets the jettisoned back into all,
tasting, each being a tongue,
vague umbrations of chemical:
this way thrilling, that way Wrong,

the pure always inimical,
compound being even the sheer thing
I suspend I in, and thrust
against, for speed and feeding,
all earblades for the eel's wave-gust
over crayfishes' unpressured beading,
for bird-dive boom, redfin's gaped gong –

Cattle Ancestor

Darrambawli and all his wives, they came feeding from the south
    east
back in that first time. Darrambawli is a big red fellow,
terrible fierce. He scrapes up dust, singing, whirling his bullroarers
in the air: he swings them and they sing out Crack! Crack!
All the time he's mounting his women, all the time more *kulka*,
more, more, smelling their *kulka* and looking down his nose.
Kangaroo and emu mobs run from him, as he tears up their shelters,
throwing the people in the air, stamping out their fires.
Darrambawli gathers up his brothers, all making that sad cry *mar
    mar:*
he initiates his brothers, the Bulluktruk. They walk head down
    in a line
and make the big blue ranges. You hear their clinking noise in there.
Darrambawli has wives everywhere, he has to gallop back and forth,
mad for their *kulka*. You see him on the coast, and on the plains.
They're eating up the country, so the animals come to spear them:
You have to die now, you're starving us. But then Waark the crow
tells Darrambawli Your wives, they're spearing them. He is
    screaming,
frothing at the mouth, that's why his chest is all white nowadays.
Jerking two knives, he screams *I make new waterholes! I bring the best
    song!*
He makes war on all that mob, raging, dotting the whole country.
He frightens the water-snakes; they run away, they can't sit down.
The animals forget how to speak. There is only one song
for a while. Darrambawli must sing it on his own.

Mollusc

By its nobship sailing upside down,
by its inner sexes, by the crystalline
pimplings of its skirts, by the sucked-on
lifelong kiss of its toppling motion,
by the viscose optics now extruded
now wizened instantaneously, by the
ridges grating up a food-path, by
the pop shell in its nick of dry,
by excretion, the earthworm coils, the glibbing,
by the gilt slipway, and by pointing
perhaps as far back into time as
ahead, a shore being folded interior,
by boiling on salt, by coming uncut over
a razor's edge, by hiding the Oligocene
underleaf may this and every snail sense
itself ornament the weave of presence.

The Snake's Heat Organ

Earth after sun is slow burn
as eye scales darken.
                    Water's no-burn.
Smaller sunlives all dim slowly
to predawn invisibility
but self-digesters constantly glow-burn.
Their blood-coals fleet
                    glimmering as I spin
lightly over textures.
                    Passenger of my passage
I reach round upright leaf-burners, I
reach and follow under rock balances,
I gather at the drinking margin.

Across the nothing there
                    an ardency

is lapping blank, which segments serially up
beneath the coruscating braincakes
                              into the body,
three skin-sheddings' length of no-burn negatively
coiled in a guttering chamber:
                    a fox,
it is pedalling off now,
a scintillating melon,

                    gamboge in its hull
                    round a dark seed centre
and hungry as the sun.

Yard Horse

Ripple, pond, liftoff fly. Unlid the outswallowing snorter
to switch at fly. Ripples over day's gigantic peace.
No oestrus scent, no haem, no pung of other stallion,
no frightening unsmell of sexless horses,
the unbearable pee-submissive ones who are not in instinct.
Far off blistering grass-sugars. Smoke infinitesimal in air
and, pond gone, his dense standing now would alert all mares
for herded flight. Fire crowds up-mountain swift as horses,
teeters widening down. Pond to granite to derelict
timber go the fur-textures. Large head over wire
contains faint absent tastes, sodichlor, chaff, calc.
The magnified grass is shabby in head-bowed focus, the earth
it grows from only tepidly exists, blots of shade are abyssal.
In his mind, fragments of rehearsal: lowered snaking neck
like goose-speech, to hurry mares; bounced trot-gait of menace
oncoming, with whipping headshake; poses, then digestion.
Moment to moment, his coat is a climate of mirrorings
and his body is the word for every meaning in his universe.

The Octave of Elephants

Bull elephants, when not weeping need, wander soberly alone.
Only females congregate and talk, in a seismic baritone:

Dawn and sundown we honour you, Jehovah Brahm,
who allow us to intone our ground bass in towering calm.

Inside the itchy fur of life is the sonorous planet Stone
which we hear and speak through, depending our flugelhorn.

Winds barrel, waves shunt shore, earth moans in ever-construction
being hurried up the sky, against weight, by endless suction.

We are two species, male and female. Bulls run to our call.
We converse. They weep, and announce, but rarely talk at all.

As presence resembles everything, our bulls reflect its solitude
and we, suckling, blaring, hotly loving, reflect its motherhood.

Burnt-maize-smelling Death, who brings the collapse-sound
  bum-bum,
has embryos of us on its free limbs: four legs and a thumb.

From dusting our newborn with puffs, we assume a boggling pool
into our heads, to re-silver each other's wrinkles and be cool.

Pigs

Us all on sore cement was we.
Not warmed then with glares. Not glutting mush
under that pole the lightning's tied to.
No farrow-shit in milk to make us randy.
Us back in cool god-shit. We ate crisp.
We nosed up good rank in the tunnelled bush.
Us all fuckers then. And Big, huh? Tusked
the balls-biting dog and gutsed him wet.

Us shoved down the soft cement of rivers.
Us snored the earth hollow, filled farrow, grunted.
Never stopped growing. We sloughed, we soughed
and balked no weird till the high ridgebacks was us
with weight-buried hooves. Or bristly, with milk.
Us never knowed like slitting nor hose-biff then.
Not the terrible body-cutting screams up ahead.
The burnt water kicking. This gone-already feeling
here in no place with our heads on upside down.

The Cows on Killing Day

All me are standing on feed. The sky is shining.

All me have just been milked. Teats all tingling still
from that dry toothless sucking by the chilly mouths
that gasp loudly in in in, and never breathe out.

All me standing on feed, move the feed inside me.
One me smells of needing the bull, that heavy urgent me,
the back-climber, who leaves me humped, straining, but light
and peaceful again, with crystalline moving inside me.

Standing on wet rock, being milked, assuages the calf-sorrow in me.
Now the me who needs mounts on me, hopping, to signal the bull.

The tractor comes trotting in its grumble; the heifer human
bounces on top of it, and cud comes with the tractor,
big rolls of tight dry feed: lucerne, clovers, buttercup, grass,
that's been bitten but never swallowed, yet is cud.
She walks up over the tractor and down it comes, roll on roll
and all me following, eating it, and dropping the good pats.

The heifer human smells of needing the bull human
and is angry. All me look nervously at her
as she chases the dog me dream of horning dead: our enemy
of the light loose tongue. Me'd jam him in his squeals.

Me, facing every way, spreading out over feed.

One me is still in the yard, the place skinned of feed.
Me, old and sore-boned, little milk in that me now,
licks at the wood. The oldest bull human is coming.

Me in the peed yard. A stick goes out from the human
and cracks, like the whip. Me shivers and falls down
with the terrible, the blood of me, coming out behind an ear.
Me, that other me, down and dreaming in the bare yard.

All me come running. It's like the Hot Part of the sky
that's hard to look at, this that now happens behind wood
in the raw yard. A shining leaf, like off the bitter gum tree
is with the human. It works in the neck of me
and the terrible floods out, swamped and frothy. All me make the
   Roar,
some leaping stiff-kneed, trying to horn that worst horror.
The wolf-at-the-calves is the bull human. Horn the bull human!

But the dog and the heifer human drive away all me.

Looking back, the glistening leaf is still moving.
All of dry old me is crumpled, like the hills of feed,
and a slick me like a huge calf is coming out of me.

The carrion-stinking dog, who is calf of human and wolf,
is chasing and eating little blood things the humans scatter
and all me run away, over smells, toward the sky.

Shellback Tick

Match-head   of groins
nailhead   in fur
blank   itch   of blank
the blood   thereof
is the strength thereof is
the jellied life-breath   is O the
sweet incision   so the curdy reed
floodeth sun-hot liquor the only ichor the only
thing which existeth wholly alley-echoing
duple rhythmic feed which same of great yore turned
my back on every other thing the mothering thereof
the seed whereof in need-clotting strings
of plaque I dissolve with reagent drool
that doth stagger swelling's occult throb.
O one tap of splendour turned to me —
blank years   grass grip
sun   haggard   rain
shell to that all.

Cell DNA

I am the singular
in free fall.
I and my doubles
carry it all:

life's slim volume
spirally bound.
It's what I'm about,
it's what I'm around.

Presence and hungers
imbue a sap mote
with the world as they spin it.
I teach it by rote

but its every command
was once a miscue
that something rose to,
Presence and freedom

re-wording, re-beading
strains on a strand
making I and I more different
than we could stand.

Goose to Donkey

My big friend, I bow help;
I bow Get up, big friend:
let me land-swim again beside your clicky feet,
don't sleep flat with dried wet in your holes.

Spermaceti

I sound my sight, and flexing skeletons eddy
in our common wall. With a sonic bolt from the fragrant
chamber of my head, I burst the lives of some
and slow, backwashing them into my mouth. I lighten,
breathe, and laze below again. And peer in long low tones
over the curve of Hard to river-tasting and oil-tasting
coasts, to the grand grinding coasts of rigid air.
How the wall of our medium has a shining, pumping rim:
the withstood crush of deep flight in it, perpetual entry!
Only the holes of eyesight and breath still tie us
to the dwarf-making Air, where true sight barely functions.
The power of our wall likewise guards us from
slowness of the rock Hard, its life-powdering compaction,
from its fissures and streamy layers that we sing into sight
but are silent, fixed, disjointed in. Eyesight is a leakage
of nearby into us, and shows us the tastes of food

conformed over its spines. But our greater sight is uttered.
I sing beyond the curve of distance the living joined bones
of my song-fellows; I sound a deep volcano's valve tubes
storming whitely in black weight; I receive an island's slump,
song-scrambling ship's heartbeats, and the sheer shear of current-
    forms
bracketing a seamount. The wall, which running blind I demolish,
heals, prickling me with sonars. My every long shaped cry
re-establishes the world, and centres its ringing structure.

Migratory

I am the nest that comes and goes,
I am the egg that isn't now,
I am the beach, the food in sand,
the shade with shells and the shade with sticks.
I am the right feeling on washed shine,
in wing-lifting surf, in running about
beak-focused: the feeling of here, that stays
and stays, then lengthens out over
the hill of hills and the feedy sea.
I am the wrongness of here, when it
is true to fly along the feeling
the length of its great rightness, while days
burn from vast to a gold gill in the dark
to vast again, for many feeds
and floating rests, till the sun ahead
becomes the sun behind, and half
the little far days of the night are different.
Right feelings of here arrive with me:
I am the nests danced for and now,
I am the crying heads to fill,
I am the beach, the sand in food,
the shade with sticks and the double kelp shade.

Home Suite

Home is the first
and final poem
and every poem between
has this mum home seam.

Home's the weakest enemy
as iron steams starch –
but to war against home
is the longest march.

Home has no neighbours.
They are less strong
than the tree, or the sideboard.
All who come back belong.

No later first-class plane
flies the sad quilt wings.
Any feeling after final
must be home, with idyll-things.

Love may be a recent,
and liquid enough term
to penetrate and mollify
what's compact in home.

The Wedding at Berrico

Christina and James, 8 February 1992

To reach your watershed country
we've driven this summer's green climbs
and the creekwater film spooling over
causeways got spliced many times
with its boulders like ice under whisky,
tree pools mirrory as the eyes of horses.

Great hills above, the house *en fête*:
we've parked between soaring rhymes
and slipped in among brilliant company.

Here are your gifts. I see God's sent
all your encounters so far with him:
life. Landscape. Unfraught love. Some poetry.
Risk too, with his star rigger Freedom,
but here's poise, for whatever may come.
What's life wish you? Sound genetics, delight,
long resilience against gravity, the sight
of great-grandchildren, a joint sense of home.

Hey, all these wishes in smart boxes! Fun,
challenges, Meaning, work-satisfaction –
this must be the secular human lot: health
till high old age, children of character,
dear friendships. And the testing one: wealth.
Quietly we add ours: may you
always have each other, and want to.

Few poems I've made mention our children.
That I write at all got you dork names.
More might have brought worse. Our jealous nation . . .
I am awed at you, though, today,
silk restraining your briskness and gumption,
my mother's face still hauntingly in yours

and this increase, this vulnerable beauty.
James is worthy of his welcome to our family.
Never would I do, or he ask
me to do what no parental memories
could either: I won't give you away.

But now you join hands, exchanging
the vows that cost joyfully dear.
They move you to the centre of life
and us gently to the rear.

Crankshaft

Buildings, like all made things
that can't be taken back
into the creating mind,
persist as reefs of the story
which made them, and which someone
will try to drive out of fashion.

On a brown serpentine road,
cornice around a contour
into steep kikuyu country,
the Silver Farm appears
hard-edged on its scarp of green
long-ago rainforest mountain.

All its verandahs walled in,
the house, four-square to a pyramid
point, like an unhit spike head
bulks white above the road
and the dairy and cowyard
are terraced above, to let
all liquid waste good spill down
around windowless small sheds, iron
or board, alike metallised with silverfrost,
to studded orange trees, hen-coops,
wire netting smoky with peas,
perched lettuce, tomato balconies.

The story that gathers into
such pauses of shape isn't often
told to outsiders, or in words.
It might be poisoned by your hearing it,
thinking it just a story.
It is for its own characters
and is itself a character.

The Silver Farm has always been
self-sufficient, ordering little in.

Two brothers and respective wives
and children, once, live there quietly
in the one house. At dawn,
the milking done, the standing wife
knits by the roadside, watching
small spacy-eyed caramel Jersey
cows graze the heavy verges,
and the sitting wife, on a folding stool
hidden by her blanket, reads
two turns of the road further on.
Men, glimpsed above in the dairy,
flit through the python fig tree.

　　A syphoned dam, a mesh room —
　　and the Silver Farm closes
　　behind a steep escutcheon pasture
　　charged with red deer. New people:
　　unknown story. Past there
　　is where the lightning struggled
　　all over the night sky like bared Fact
　　ripping free of its embodiments, and
　　pronged the hillside, turning
　　a rider on his numbed horse
　　to speechless, for minutes, rubber.

Above is a shrine house, kept
in memory of deep childhood
whitewash-raw, as it always was
despite prosperity. No stories
cling to the mother, many
to the irascible yeoman heir
blown by a huff, it seems his own,
a lifetime's leap from Devonshire:
Quiet, woman, I am master here!

　　No high school for our boys:
　　it would make them restless.
　　Children of this regimen,
　　touchy well-informed cattlemen
　　and their shrine-tending sister

remember their father's pride
in knowing all of Pope by heart:
Recited those poems till he died!
The proper study of mankind
is weakness. If good were not
the weaker side, how would
we know to choose it?

Shrine-houses are common here,
swept on visits, held
out of time by feeling.
I leave this one's real story
up its private road, where
it abrades and is master.
I'm glad to be not much deeper
than old gossip in it. Fiction-deep.
A reverence for closed boxes is returning.
Left standing, still grouped readably
in the countryside, with trees,
they may be living communities.

How does the house of the man
who won his lands in a card game
come to have the only slate roof
in all these hills? Was it
in hopes of such arrived style
that when the cards' leadlight smile
brightened, his way, his drawl didn't
waver, under iron and tongue-and-groove?
No one knows. He attracted no yarns.
Since all stories are of law, any
about him might have rebounded,
like bad whisky, inside the beloved losers.

Keenly as I read detective fiction
I've never cared who done it.
I read it for the ambiences:
David Small reasoning rabbinically,
Jim Chee playing tapes in his tribal
patrol car to learn the Blessing Way,

or the tweed antiquaries of London,
fog from the midriff down,
discoursing with lanthorn and laudanum.

    I read it, then, for the stretches
    of presence. And to watch analysis
    and see how far author and sleuth
    can transcend that, submitting
    to the denied whole mind, and admit it,
    since the culprit's always the same:
    the poetry. Someone's poem did it.

This further hill throws another
riffle of cuttings, and a vista
sewn with fences, chinked with dams
and the shed-free, oddly placed
brick houses of the urban people
who will be stories if they stay.

    There's a house that was dying
    of moss, sun-bleach and piety –
    probate and guitar tunes revived it.
    Down the other way, seawards, dawn's way,
    a house that was long alive
    is sealed. Nailgunned shut
    since the morning after its last day.

And it was such an open house:
You stepped from the kitchen table's
cards and beer, or a meal of ingredients
in the old unmixed style, straight
off lino into the gaze of cattle
and sentimental dogs, and beloved
tall horses, never bet on. This was
a Turf house: that is, it bet on men.
Men sincere and dressy as detectives
who could make time itself run dead.

    Gaunt posthumous wood that supported
    the rind-life of trees still stands

on that property. The house is walled
in such afterlife sawn. Inside it
are the afterlives of clothes, of plates,
equestrienne blue ribbons, painted photos,
of childlessness and privacy.
Beef-dark tools and chain out in the sheds
are being pilfered back into the present.

Plaintive with those she could
make into children, and shrewd
with those she couldn't, the lady
sits beautifully, in the pride
of her underlip, shy of naming names
as that other lot, the Irish, she canters
mustering on Timoshenko with a twig of leaves.

When urban dollars were already
raining on any country acre, her husband
with the trickle of smoke to his wall eye
from his lip-screw of tobacco
sold paddocks to a couple of nephews.

The arm a truck had shattered
to a crankshaft long ago trembled,
signing. He charged a fifth of what
he could have. A family price,
and used the grazing rights,
which we had thrown in, to make sure
we didn't too greatly alter
their parents' landscape till he
and she were finished with it.

Now they, who were cool midday East
to my childhood, have moved on into
the poem that can't be read
till you yourself are in it.

The Family Farmers' Victory

for Salvatore Zofrea

White grist that turned people black,
it was the white cane sugar
fixed humans as black or white. Sugar,
first luxury of the modernising poor.

It turned slavery black to repeat it.
Black to grow sugar, white to eat it
shuffled all the tropic world. Cane sugar
would only grow in sweat of the transported.

That was the old plantation,
blackbirding ship to commissar.
White teeth decried the tyranny of sugar –
but Italian Australians finished it.

On the red farm blocks they bought
and cleared, for cane-besieged stilt houses
between rain-smoky hills on the Queensland shore,
they made the black plantation obsolete.

When they come, we still et creamed spaghetti cold, for pudding,
and we didn't want their Black Hand on our girls.
But they ploughed, burnt, lumped cane: it shimmied like a
    gamecock's tail.
Then the wives come out, put up with flies, heat, crocodiles,
    Irish clergy,
and made shopkeepers learn their lingo. Stubborn Australian
    shopkeepers.
L'abito, signora, voletelo in saia, do you?
Serge suits in Queensland? Course. You didn't let the white side
    down.

Shorts, pasta, real coffee. English only at school. But sweet biscuits,
cakes, icing – we learnt all that off the British and we loved it!
Big families, aunts, cousins. You slept like a salt tongue, in gauze.
Cool was under the mango tree. Walls of cane enclosed us and fell:

sudden slant-slashed vistas, burnt bitter caramel. Our pink roads
were partings in a world of haircut. I like to go back. It's
    changed now.
After thirty years, even Sicilians let their daughters work in town.

Cane work was too heavy for children
so these had their childhoods
as not all did, on family farms,
before full enslavement of machines.

But of grown-up hundreds on a worked estate
still only one of each sex can be adult.
Likewise factory, and office, and concern:
any employee's a child, in the farmer's opinion.

Dead Trees in the Dam

Castle scaffolding tall in moat,
the dead trees in the dam
flower each morning with birds.

It can be just the three resident
cormorants with musket-hammer necks, plus
the clinician spoonbill, its long pout;

twilight's herons who were almost too lightfoot
to land; pearl galahs in pink-fronted
confederacy, each starring in its frame,

or it may be a misty candelabrum
of egrets lambent before saint Sleep –
who gutter awake and balance stiffly off.

Odd mornings, it's been all bloodflag
and rifle green: a stopped-motion shrapnel
of kingparrots. Smithereens when they freaked.

Rarely, it's wed ducks, whose children
will float among the pillars. In daytime
magpies sidestep up wood to jag pinnacles

and the big blow-in cuckoo crying
Alarm, Alarm on the wing is not let light.
This hours after dynastic charts of high

profile ibis have rowed away to beat
the paddocks. Which, however green, are
always watercolour, and on brown paper.

Rock Music

Sex is a Nazi. The students all knew
this at your school. To it, everyone's subhuman
for parts of their lives. Some are all their lives.
You'll be one of those if these things worry you.

The beautiful Nazis, why are they so cruel?
Why, to castrate the aberrant, the original, the wounded
who might change our species and make obsolete
the true race. Which is those who never leave school.

For the truth, we are silent. For the flattering dream,
in massed farting reassurance, we spasm and scream,
but what is a Nazi but sex pitched for crowds?

It's the Calvin SS: you are what you've got
and you'll wrinkle and fawn and work after you're shot
though tears pour in secret from the hot indoor clouds.

The Rollover

Some of us primary producers, us farmers and authors
are going round to watch them evict a banker.
It'll be sad. I hate it when the toddlers and wives
are out beside the fence, crying, and the big kids
wear that thousand-yard stare common in all refugees.
Seeing home desecrated as you lose it can do that to you.

There's the ute piled high with clothes and old debentures.
There's the faithful VDU, shot dead, still on its lead.
This fellow's dad and grandad were bankers before him, they
    sweated
through the old hard inspections, had years of brimming foreclosure,
but here it all ends. He'd lent three quarters and only
asked for a short extension. Six months. But you have to

line the drawer somewhere. You have to be kind to be cruel.
It's Sydney or the cash these times. Who buys the Legend of the
    Bank
any more? The laconic teller, the salt-of-the-earth branch
    accountant
it's all an Owned Boys story. Now they reckon he's grabbed a gun
and an old coin sieve and holed up in the vault, screaming
about his years of work, his identity. Queer talk from a bank-
    johnny!

We're catching flak, too, from a small mob of his mates,
inbred under-manager types, here to back him up. Troublemakers,
land-despoiling white trash. It'll do them no good. Their turn
is coming. They'll be rationalised themselves, made adapt
to a multinational society. There's no room in that for privileged
traditional ways of life. No land rights for bankers.

Late Summer Fires

The paddocks shave black
with a foam of smoke that stays,
welling out of red-black wounds.

In the white of a drought
this happens. The hardcourt game.
Logs that fume are mostly cattle,

inverted, stubby. Tree stumps are kilns.
Walloped, wiped, hand-pumped,
even this day rolls over, slowly.

At dusk, a family drives sheep
out through the yellow
of the Aboriginal flag.

Corniche

I work all day and hardly drink at all.
I can reach down and feel if I'm depressed.
I adore the Creator because I made myself
and a few times a week a wire jags in my chest.

The first time, I'd been coming apart all year,
weeping, incoherent; cigars had given me up;
any road round a cliff edge I'd whimper along in low gear
then: cardiac horror. Masking my pulse's calm lub-dup.

It was the victim-sickness. Adrenalin howling in my head,
the black dog was my brain. Come to drown me in my breath
was energy's black hole, depression, compère of the predawn show
when, returned from a pee, you stew and welter in your death.

The rogue space rock is on course to snuff your world,
sure. But go acute, and its oncoming fills your day.
The brave die but once? I could go a hundred times a week,
clinging to my pulse with the world's edge inches away.

Laugh, who never shrank around wizened genitals there
or killed themselves to stop dying. The blow that never falls
batters you stupid. Only gradually do
you notice a slight scorn in you for what appals.

A self inside self, cool as conscience, one to be erased
in your final night, or faxed, still knows beneath
all the mute grand opera and uncaused effect –
that death which can be imagined is not true death.

The crunch is illusion. There's still no outside world
but you start to see. You're like one enthralled by bad art –
yet for a real onset, what cover! You gibber to Casualty,
are checked, scorned, calmed. There's nothing wrong with your
    heart.

The terror of death is not afraid of death.
Fear, pure, is intransitive. A Hindenburg of vast rage
rots, though, above your life. See it, and you feel flogged
but like an addict you sniffle aboard, to your cage,

because you will cling to this beast as it gnaws you,
for the crystal in its kidneys, the elixir in its wings,
till your darlings are the police of an immense fatigue.
I came to the world unrehearsed but I've learned some things.

When you curl, stuffed, in the pot at rainbow's end
it is life roaring and racing and nothing you can do.
Were you really God you could have lived all the lives
that now decay into misery and cripple you.

A for adrenalin, the original A–bomb, fuel
and punishment of aspiration, the Enlightenment's air-burst.
Back when God made me, I had no script. It was better.
For all the death, we also die unrehearsed.

Suspended Vessels

for Joanna Gooding and Simon Curtis

Here is too narrow and brief:
equality and justice, to be real,
require the timeless. It argues
afterlife even to name them.

I've thought this more since that morning
in barren country vast as space-time
but affluent with cars
at the fence where my tightening budget
denied me basket-room
under the haunches of a hot-air balloon

and left thirteen people in it,
all ages, teens to grans,
laughing excitedly as the dragon nozzle
exhaled hoarse blazing lift, tautening it,
till they grabbed, dragged, swayed
up, up into their hiatus.

Others were already aloft
I remember, lightbulbs against the grizzled
mountain ridge and bare sky,
vertical yachts, with globe spinnakers.

More were being rigged, or offering
their gape for gusts of torch.
I must have looked away —
suddenly a cry erupted everywhere:

two, far up, lay overlapping,
corded and checked as the foresails of a ship
but tangled, and one collapsing.

I suppress in my mind
the long rag unravelling, the mixed
high voice of its spinning fall,

the dust-blast crash, the privacies
and hideous equality without justice
of those thirteen, which running helpers,
halting, must have seen
and professionals lifted out.

Instead, I look at coloured cash and plastic
and toddlerhood's vehement equities
that are never quite silenced.
Indeed, it prickles, and soon glares
if people do not voice them.

The Water Column

We had followed the catwalk upriver
by flowering trees and granite sheer
to the Basin park crying with peacocks.

After those, we struck human conversation.
A couple we'd thought Austrian proved to be
Cape Coloured. Wry good sense and lore

and love of their strange country
they presented us with, cheerfully.
They were eager 'to get home for the riots'.

As we talked, shoes dreamily, continually
passed above us on the horizontal chairlift.
It was Blundstones and joggers that year,

cogwheel treads with faces between them.
That was also the year I learned
the Basin was a cold crater lake:

swimmers whacking above ancient drownings –
'it's never been plumbed, in places'.
I thought of a rock tube of water

down, down levels too frigid for upwelling,
standing at last on this miles-deep
lager head, above a live steam layer

in impossible balance, facing
where there can't be water, the planet's
convecting inner abortive iron star.

The Beneficiaries

Higamus hogamus
Western intellectuals
never praise Auschwitz.
Most ungenerous. Most odd,
when they claim it's what finally
won them their centuries-
long war against God.

Wallis Lake Estuary

for Valerie

A long street of all blue windows,
the estuary bridge is double-humped
like a bullock yoke. The north tide
teems through to four arriving rivers,
the south tide works the sinus channel
to the big heart-shaped real estate lake.
Both flood oyster farms like burnt floor joists
that islands sleep out among like dogs.

Glorious on a brass day the boiling up
from the south, of a storm above these paddocks
of shoal-creamed, wake-dolphined water.
Equally at dusk, when lamps and pelicans
are posted, the persistence of dark lands
out there on the anodised light void.

On Home Beaches

Back, in my fifties, fatter than I was then,
I step on the sand, belch down slight horror to walk
a wincing pit edge, waiting for the pistol shot
laughter. Long greening waves cash themselves, foam change
sliding into Ocean's pocket. She turns: ridicule looks down,
strappy, with faces averted, or is glare and families.
The great hawk of the beach is outstretched, point to point,
quivering and hunting. Cars are the surf at its back.
You peer, at this age, but it's still there, ridicule,
the pistol that kills women, that gets them killed, crippling men
on the towel-spattered sand. Equality is dressed, neatly,
with mouth still shut. Bared body is not equal ever.
Some are smiled to each other. Many surf, swim, play ball:
like that red boy, holding his wet T-shirt off his breasts.

On the Present Slaughter of Feral Animals

It seems that merciless human rearrangement
of the whole earth is to have no green ending.
In khaki where nothing shoots back, rangers pose,
entering a helicopter with its sniping door removed.
In minutes, they are over drab where buffalo flee
ahead of dust – beasts rotund and beetle brown, with rayed

handlebar horns – or over shine that hobbles them in spray.
The rifle arrests one's gallop, and one more, and one,
cow, calf, bull, the two tons of projectile
power riding each bullet's invisible star
whipcrack their plunging fluids. Poor caked Asian cattle,
they lie, successive, like towns of salt stench on a map.

Passionate with altruism as ever inquisition was,
a statistical dream loads up for donkeys, cats, horses.
The slab-fed military rifles, with lenses tubed on top,
open and shut. A necked bulging cartridge case and animal

both spin to oblivion. Behind an ear, fur flicks,
and an unknowable headlong world is abolished.

But so far as treetops or humans now alive know
all these are indigenous beings. When didn't we have them?
Each was born on this continent. Burn-off pick and dusty shade
were in their memory, not chill fall, not spiced viridian.
Us against species for bare survival may justify
the infecting needle, the pig rifle up eroded gullies,

but this luxury massacre on landscapes draining of settlement
smells of gas theory. The last thing brumby horses hear
is that ideological sound, the baby boom.
It is the hidden music of a climaxing native self-hatred
where we edge unseeing around flyblown millions toward
a nonviolent dreamtime where no one living has been.

Memories of the Height-to-Weight Ratio

I was a translator in the Institute back
when being accredited as a poet
meant signing things against Vietnam.
For scorn of the bargain I wouldn't do it.

And the Institute was after me
to lose seven teeth and five stone in weight
and pass their medical. Three years I dodged
then offered the teeth under sacking threat.

From five to nine, in warm Lane Cove,
and five to nine again at night,
an irascible Carpatho-Ruthenian strove
with ethnic teeth. He claimed the bite

of a human determined their intelligence.
More gnash-power sent the brain more blood.
In Hungarian, Yiddish or Serbo-Croat
he lectured emotional fur-trimmers good,

clacking a jointed skull in his hand
and sent them to work face-numbed and bright.
This was my wife's family dentist. He
looked into my mouth, blenched at the sight,

eclipsed me with his theory of occlusion
and wrested and tugged. Pausing to blow
out cigarette smoke, he'd bite his only
accent-free mother tongue and return below

to raise my black fleet of sugar-barques
so anchored that they gave him tennis elbow.
Seven teeth I gave that our babies might eat
when students were chanting Make Love! Hey Ho!

But there was a line called Height-to-Weight
and a parallel line on Vietnam. When a tutor
in politics failed all who crossed that, and wasn't
dismissed, scholarship was back to holy writ.

Fourteen pounds were a stone, and of great yore so,
but the doctor I saw next had no schoolyard in him:
You're a natural weight-lifter! Come join my gym!
Sonnets of flesh could still model my torso.

Modernism's not modern: it's police and despair.
I wear it as fat, and it gnawed off my hair
as my typewriter clicked over gulfs and birch spaces
where the passive voice muffled enormity and faces.

But when the Institute started afresh
to circle my job, we decamped to Europe
and spent our last sixpence on a pig's head.
Any job is a comedown, where I was bred.

Like Wheeling Stacked Water

Dried nests in the overhanging limbs
are where the flood hatched eggs of swirl.
Like is unscary milder love. More can be in it.

The flood boomed up nearly to the door
like a taxiing airliner. It flew past all day.
Now the creek is down to barley colour
waist deep on her, chest on him,
wearing glasses all around them, barely pushing.

Down under stops of deadwood pipe in living
branches, they move on again. The bottom
is the sunk sand cattle-road they know
but hidden down cool, and mincing
magically away at every step, still going.

The wide creek is a tree hall decorated
with drowned and tobacco ribbons,
with zippy tilting birds, with dried snakes hanging
over the doorways everywhere along.

They push on. *Say this log I'm walking*
under the water's a mast like off a
olden day ship – . Fine hessian shade
is moistening down off cross-trees,

and like wings, the rocking waterline
gloving up and down their bodies
pumps support to their swimmy planet steps.

They've got a hook and bits
of bluebottle line from salt holidays.
They had a poor worm, and crickets automatic in a jar
but they let all them off fishing.

They're taking like to an adventure instead,
up past where the undercut bank

makes that bottling noise, and the kingfisher's
beak is like the weight he's thrown by
to fly him straight.

By here, they're wheeling stacked–up water.
It has mounted like mild ice bedclothes to
their chest and chin. They have to tiptoe
under all the white davits of the bush.

But coming to the island, that is like the pupil
in acres of eye, their clothes pour water
off like heavy chain. They toil, and lighten
as they go up on it. All this is like the past
but none of it is sad. It has never ended.

It Allows a Portrait in Line Scan at Fifteen

He retains a slight 'Martian' accent, from the years of single phrases.
He no longer hugs to disarm. It is gradually allowing him affection.
It does not allow proportion. Distress is absolute, shrieking, and
    runs him at frantic speed through crashing doors.
He likes cyborgs. Their taciturn power, with his intonation.
It still runs him around the house, alone in the dark, cooing and
    laughing.
He can read about soils, populations and New Zealand. On
    neutral topics he's illiterate.
Arnie Schwarzenegger is an actor. He isn't a cyborg really, is he, Dad?
He lives on forty acres, with animals and trees, and used to draw
    it continually.
He knows the map of Earth's fertile soils, and can draw it freehand.
He can only lie in a panicked shout *SorrySorryIdidn'tdoit!* warding
    off conflict with others and himself.
When he ran away constantly it was to the greengrocers to
    worship stacked fruit.
His favourite country was the Ukraine: it is nearly all deep fertile
    soil.
Giggling, he climbed all over the dim Freudian psychiatrist who
    told us how autism resulted from 'refrigerator' parents.

When asked to smile, he photographs a rictus-smile on his face.

It long forbade all naturalistic films. They were Adult movies.

If they (that is, he) *are bad the police will put them in hospital.*

He sometimes drew the farm amid Chinese or Balinese rice terraces.

When a runaway, he made uproar in the police station, playing
at three times adult speed.

Only animated films were proper. *Who Framed Roger Rabbit* then
authorised the rest.

Phrases spoken to him he would take as teaching, and repeat.

When he worshipped fruit, he screamed as if poisoned when it
was fed to him.

A one-word first conversation: *Blane. – Yes! Plane, that's right,
baby! – Blane.*

He has forgotten nothing, and remembers the precise quality of
experiences.

It requires rulings: *Is stealing very playing up, as bad as murder?*

He counts at a glance, not looking. And he has never been lost.

When he ate only nuts and dried fruit, words were for dire
emergencies.

He knows all the breeds of fowls, and the counties of Ireland.

He'd begun to talk, then returned to babble, then silence. It
withdrew speech for years.

When he took your hand, it was to work it, as a multi-purpose
tool.

He is anger's mirror, and magnifies any near him, raging it down.

It still won't allow him fresh fruit, or orange juice with bits in it.

He swam in the midwinter dam at night. It had no rules about cold.

He was terrified of thunder and finally cried as if in explanation *It
– angry!*

He grilled an egg he'd broken into bread. Exchanges of soil-
knowledge are called landtalking.

He lives in objectivity. I was sure Bell's palsy would leave my
face only when he said it had begun to.

Don't say word! when he was eight forbade the word 'autistic' in
his presence.

Bantering questions about girlfriends cause a terrified look and
blocked ears.

He sometimes centred the farm in a furrowed American Midwest.

Eye contact, Mum! means he truly wants attention. It dislikes
I-contact.

He is equitable and kind, and only ever a little jealous. It was a
  relief when that little arrived.
He surfs, bowls, walks for miles. For many years he hasn't trailed
  his left arm while running.
I gotta get smart! looking terrified into the years. *I gotta get smart!*

Performance

I starred last night, I shone:
I was footwork and firework in one,

a rocket that wriggled up and shot
darkness with a parasol of brilliants
and a peewee descant on a flung bit;
I was busters of glitter-bombs expanding
to mantle and aurora from a crown,
I was fouettés, falls of blazing paint,
para-flares spot-welding cloudy heaven,
loose gold off fierce toeholds of white,
a finale red-tongued as a haka leap:
that too was a butt of all right!

As usual after any triumph, I was
of course inconsolable.

Second Childhood Is Legal

A primary teacher taking courses,
he loved the little girls,
never hard enough to be sacked:
parents made him change schools.

When sure this was his life sentence,
he dropped studies for routine:

the job, the Turf papers, beer,
the then-new poker machine.

Always urbane, he boarded happily
among show-jump ribbons, nailed towels,
stockwhip attitudes he'd find reasons for
and a paddock view, with fowls.

Because the old days weren't connected
the boss wouldn't have the phone.
The wife loved cards, outings, *Danny Boy,*
sweet malice in a mourning tone.

Life had set his hosts aside, as a couple,
from verve or parenthood.
How they lived as a threesome enlivened them
and need not be understood.

Euchre hands that brushed away the decades
also fanned rumour
and mothers of daughters banned the teacher
in his raceday humour,

but snap brim feigning awe of fat-cattle brim
and the henna rinse between them
enlarged each of the three to the others, till
the boss fell on his farm.

Alone together then, beyond the talk,
he'd cook, and tint, and curl,
and sit voluble through rare family visits
to his aged little girl.

As she got lost in the years
where she would wander,
her boy would hold her in bed
and wash sheets to spread under.

But when her relations carried her,
murmuring, out to their van,

he fled that day, as one with no rights,
as an unthanked old man.

Inside Ayers Rock

Inside Ayers Rock is lit
with paired fluorescent lights
on steel pillars supporting the ceiling
of haze-blue marquee cloth
high above the non-slip pavers.
Curving around the cafeteria
throughout vast inner space
is a Milky Way of plastic chairs
in foursomes around tables
all the way to the truck drivers' enclave.
Dusted coolabah trees grow to the ceiling,
TVs talk in gassy colours, and
round the walls are Outback shop fronts:
the Beehive Bookshop for brochures,
Casual Clobber, the bottled Country Kitchen
and the sheet-iron Dreamtime Experience
that is turned off at night.

A high bank of medal-ribbony
lolly jars presides over
island counters like opened crates,
one labelled White Mugs, and covered with them.
A two-dimensional policeman
discourages shoplifting of gifts
and near the entrance, where you pay
for fuel, there stands a tribal man
in rib-paint and pubic tassel.
It is all gentle and kind.
In beyond the children's playworld
there are fossils, like crumpled
old drawings of creatures in rock.

Contested Landscape at Forsayth

The conquest of fire-culture
on that timber countryside
has broadcast innumerable
termite mounds all through
the gravel gold rush hills
and the remnant railhead town,
petrified French mustards
out of jars long smashed.

Train platform and tin Shire
are beleaguered in nameless cemetery.
Outworks of the Dividing range
are annulled under Dreaming-turds.
It's as if every place a miner
cursed, or thought of sex,
had its abraded marker. Mile
on mile of freckled shade,
the ordinary is riddled by
cylinder-pins of unheard music.

On depopulated country
frail billions are alive
in layered earthen lace.
Their every flight is
a generation, glueing towers
which scatter and mass
on a blind smell-plan.
Cobras and meta-cobras
in the bush, immense black vines
await monsoon in a world
of clay lingam altars.

Like the monuments to every
mortal thing that a planet without God
would require, and inscriptionless
as rage would soon weather those,
the anthills erupt on verges,

on streets, round the glaring pub,
its mango trees and sleeping-fridges,
an estuary of undergrounds,
dried cities of the flying worm.

The Shield-Scales of Heraldry

Surmounting my government's high evasions
stands a barbecue of crosses and birds
tended by a kangaroo and emu
but in our courts, above the judge,
a lion and a unicorn still keep
their smaller offspring, plus a harp,
in an open prison looped with mottoes.

Coats of arms, plaster Rorschach blots,
crowned stone moths, they encrust Europe.
As God was dismissed from churches
they fluttered in and cling to the walls,
abstract comic-pages held by scrolled beasts,
or wear on the flagstones underfoot.
They pertain to an earlier Antichrist,

the one before police. Mafiose citadels
made them, states of one attended family
islanded in furrows. The oldest
are the simplest. A cross, some coins,
a stripe, a roof tree, a spur rowel,
bowstaves, a hollow-gutted lion,
and all in lucid target colours.

Under tinned heads with reveries tied on,
shields are quartered and cubed by marriage
till they are sacred campaign maps
or anatomy inside dissected mantling,
glyphs minutely clear through their one
rule, that colour must abut either
gold or silver, the non-weapon metals.

The New World doesn't blazon well –
the new world ran away from blazonry
or was sent away in chains by it –
but exceptions shine: the spread eagle
with the fireworks display on its belly
and in the thinks-balloon above its head.
And when as a half-autistic

kid in scrub paddocks vert and or
I grooved on the cloisons of pedigree
it was a vivid writing of system
that hypnotised me, beyond the obvious
euphemism of force. It was eight hundred
years of cubist art and Europe's dreamings:
the Cup, the Rose, the Ship, the Antlers.

High courage, bestial snobbery,
neither now merits ungrace from us.
They could no longer hang me,
throttling, for a rabbit sejant.
Like everyone, I would now be lord
or lady myself, and pardon me
or myself loose the coronet-necked hounds.

The Year of the Kiln Portraits

I came in from planting more trees.
I was sweating, and flopped down aslant
on the sofa. You and Clare were sitting
at the lunch table, singing as you do
in harmony even I hear as beautiful,
mezzo soprano and soprano,
for anything Arno. You winked at me
and, liquescent as my face was,
I must have looked like the year
you painted all our portraits, lovingly,
exquisitely, on ceramic tiles

in undrying oil, just one
or at most two colours at a time
and carried them braced oblique, wet,
in plastic ice-cream boxes to town.
It was encaustic painting,
ancient Rome's photography, that gets
developed in successive kiln firings
till it lives, time-freed, transposed
in behind a once-blank glaze.
Afterwards, you did some figured tiles
for our patchwork chimney, then stopped.
In art, you have serious gifts. But it's
crazy: you're not driven. Not obsessive.

Tympan Alley

Adult songs in English,
avoiding schmaltz,
pre-twang:
the last songs adults sang.

When roles and manners wore
their cuffs as shot as Or-
tega y Gasset's,
soloists sang

as if a jeweller raised
pinches of facets
for hearts as yet unfazed
by fatty assets.

Adult songs with English;
the brilliantine long-play
records of the day
sing of the singlish,

the arch from wry to rue,
of marques and just one Engel,
blue, that Dietrich played;
euphemism's last parade

with rhymes still on our side
unwilling to divide
the men from the poise,
of lackadays and lakatois –

and always you,
cool independent You,
unsnowable, au fait,
when Us were hotly two,

not lost in They.

A Lego of Driving to Sydney

Dousing the campfire with tea
you step on the pedal and mount
whip-high behind splashboard and socket.
Your burnished rims tilt and rebound
among bristling botany. Only
a day now to the Port,
to bodices in the coffee palace,
to metal-shying razors in suits
and bare ships towing out, to dress
and concentrate in the wind.

Motoring down the main roads,
fenced wheeltrack-choices in forest,
odd scored beds of gravel,
knotwood in the ground –
you will have to wrestle
hand and foot to reach Sydney
and win every fall.
River punts are respites.

Croak-oak! the horsedung roads
aren't scented any more, but tasted.
Paved road starts at Chatswood:
just one ferry then, to stringing
tramcars and curl the mo,
to palms in the wonderful hotels.

Blazing down a razorback
in slab dark, in a huge
American car of the chassis age
to rescue for pleated cushions
a staring loved one who'll sway
down every totter of the gangway
on cane legs. Petrol coupons
had to be scrounged for this one:
they have seen too much railway.

Queuing down bloody highways
all round Easter, crawling in
to the great herbed sandstone bowl
of tealeaf scrub and suburbs,
hills by Monier and Wunderlich
in kiln orange, with cracks of harbour,
coming down to miss the milking
on full board, with baked Sundays,
life now to be neat and dry eyed,
coming down to be gentrified.

One long glide down the freeway
through aromatic radar zones,
soaring Egyptian rock cuttings
bang into a newsprint-coloured
rainstorm, tweeting the car phone
about union shares and police futures.
Driving in in your thousands
to the Show, to be detained
half a lifetime, or to grow rental
under steel flagpoles lapping
with multicoloured recipes.

Burning Want

From just on puberty, I lived in funeral:
mother dead of miscarriage, father trying to be dead,
we'd boil sweat-brown cloth; cows repossessed the garden.
Lovemaking brought death, was the unuttered principle.

I met a tall adopted girl some kids thought aloof,
but she was intelligent. Her poise of white-blonde hair
proved her no kin to the squat tanned couple who loved her.
Only now do I realise she was my first love.

But all my names were fat-names, at my new town school.
Between classes, kids did erocide: destruction of sexual morale.
Mass refusal of unasked love; that works. Boys cheered as
    seventeen-
year-old girls came on to me, then ran back whinnying ridicule.

The slender girl came up on holidays from the city
to my cousins' farm. She was friendly and sane.
Whispers giggled round us. A letter was written as from me
and she was there, in mid-term, instantly.

But I called people 'the humans' not knowing it was rage.
I learned things sidelong, taking my rifle for walks,
recited every scene of *From Here to Eternity*, burned paddocks
and soldiered back each Monday to that dawning Teen age.

She I admired, and almost relaxed from placating,
was gnawed by knowing what she came from, not who.
Showing off was my one social skill, oddly never with her
but I dissembled feelings, till mine were unknown to me too

and I couldn't add my want to her shortfall of wantedness.
I had forty more years, with one dear remission,
of a white paralysis: she's attracted it's not real nothing is enough
she's mistaken she'll die go now! she'll tell any minute she'll laugh —

Whether other hands reached out to Marion, or didn't,
at nineteen in her training ward she had a fatal accident
alone, at night, they said, with a lethal injection
and was spared from seeing what my school did to the world.

The Last Hellos

Don't die, Dad —
but they die.

This last year he was wandery:
took off a new chainsaw blade
and cobbled a spare from bits.
Perhaps if I lay down
my head'll come better again.
His left shoulder kept rising
higher in his cardigan.

He could see death in a face.
Family used to call him in
to look at sick ones and say.
At his own time, he was told.

The knob found in his head
was duck-egg size. Never hurt.
Two to six months, Cecil.

I'll be right, he boomed
to his poor sister on the phone
I'll do that when I finish dyin.

★

Don't die, Cecil.
But they do.

Going for last drives
in the bush, odd massive
board–slotted stumps bony white
in whipstick second growth.
I could chop all day.

*I could always cash
a cheque, in Sydney or anywhere.
Any of the shops.*

Eating, still at the head
of the table, he now missed
food on his knife side.

*Sorry, Dad, but like
have you forgiven your enemies?
Your father and all them?*
All his lifetime of hurt.

I must have (grin). *I don't
think about that now.*

★

People can't say goodbye
any more. They say last hellos.

Going fast, over Christmas,
he'd still stumble out
of his room, where his photos
hang over the other furniture,
and play host to his mourners.

The courage of his bluster
firm big voice of his confusion.

Two last days in the hospital:
his long forearms were still
red mahogany. His hands
gripped steel frame. *I'm dyin.*

On the second day:
You're bustin to talk but
I'm too busy dyin.

★

Grief ended when he died,
the widower like soldiers who
won't live life their mates missed.

Good boy Cecil! No more Bluey dog.
No more cowtime. No more stories.
We're still using your imagination,
it was stronger than all ours.

Your grave's got littler
somehow, in the three months.
More pointy as the clay's shrivelled,
like a stuck zip in a coat.

Your cricket boots are in
the State museum! Odd letters
still come. Two more's died since you:
Annie, and Stewart. Old Stewart.

On your day there was a good crowd,
family, and people from away.
But of course a lot had gone
to their own funerals first.

Snobs mind us off religion
nowadays, if they can.
Fuck thém. I wish you God.

Comete

Uphill in Melbourne on a beautiful day
a woman was walking ahead of her hair.
Like teak oiled soft to fracture and sway
it hung to her heels and seconded her
as a pencilled retinue, an unscrolling title
to ploughland, edged with ripe rows of dress,
a sheathed wing that couldn't fly her at all,
only itself, loosely, and her spirits.
                         A largesse
of life and self, brushed all calm and out,
its abstracted attempts on her mouth weren't seen,
nor its showering, its tenting. Just the detail
that swam in its flow-lines, glossing about –
as she paced on, comet-like, face to the sun.

Cotton Flannelette

Shake the bed, the blackened child whimpers,
O shake the bed! through beak lips that never
will come unwry. And wearily the ironframed
mattress, with nodding crockery bulbs,
jinks on its way.
                         Her brothers and sister take
shifts with the terrible glued-together baby
when their unsleeping absolute mother
reels out to snatch an hour, back to stop
the rocking and wring pale blue soap-water
over nude bladders and blood-webbed chars.

Even their cranky evasive father
is awed to stand watches rocking the bed.
Lids frogged shut, *O please shake the bed*,
her contour whorls and braille tattoos
from where, in her nightdress, she flared
out of hearth-drowse to a marrow shriek

pedalling full tilt firesleeves in mid air,
                    are grainier with repair
than when the doctor, crying *Dear God, woman!*
No one can save that child. Let her go!
spared her the treatments of the day.

Shake the bed. Like: count phone poles, rhyme,
classify realities, bang the head, any
iteration that will bring, in the brain's forks,
the melting molecules of relief,
and bring them again.
                    O rock the bed!
Nibble water with bared teeth, make lymph
like arrowroot gruel, as your mother grips you
for weeks in the untrained perfect language,
till the doctor relents. Salves and wraps you
in dressings that will be the fire again,
ripping anguish off agony,
                    and will confirm
the ploughland ridges, the gum joins
in your woman's skin, child saved by rhythm
for the sixty more years your family weaves you
on devotion's loom, rick-racking the bed
as you yourself, six years old, instruct them.

The Warm Rain

Against the darker trees or an open car shed
is where we first see rain, on a cumulous day,
a subtle slant locating the light in air
in front of a Forties still of tubs and bike-frames.

Next sign, the dust that was white pepper bared
starts pitting and re-knotting into peppercorns.
It stops being a raceway of rocket smoke behind cars,
it sidles off foliage, darkens to a lustre. The roof
of the bush barely leaks yet, but paper slows right down.

Hurrying parcels pearl but don't now split
crossing the carparks. People clap things in odd salute
to the side of their heads, yell wit, dance on their doubles.
The sunny parallels, when opposite the light, have a flung look
like falling seed. They mass, and develop a shore sound;
fixtures get cancelled, the muckiest shovels rack up.

The highway whizzes, and lorries put spin on vapour;
soon puddles hit at speed will arch over you like a slammed sea.
I love it all, I agree with it. At nightfall, the cause
of the whole thing revolves, in white and tints, on TV
like the Crab nebula; it brandishes palm trees like mops,
its borders swell over the continent, they compress the other
nations of the weather. Fruit bumps lawn, and every country dam

brews under bubbles, milky temperas sombering to oils.
Grass rains upward; the crêpe-myrtle tree heels, sopping crimson,
needing to be shaken like the kilt of a large man.
Hills run, air and paddocks are swollen. Eaves dribble like jaws
and coolness is a silent film, starring green and mirrors.
Tiny firetail finches, quiet in our climber rose, agree to it
like early humans. Cattle agree harder, hunched out in the clouds.
From here, the ocean may pump up and up and explode
around the lighthouses in gigantic cloak sleeves, the whole book
of foam slide and fritter, disclosing a pen shaft. Paratroops

of salt water may land in dock streets, skinless balloons
be flat out to queue down every drain, and the wind race
thousands of flags. Or we may be just chirpings, damped
under calm high cornfields of pour, with butter clearings

that spread and resume glare, hiding the warm rain
back inside our clothes, as mauve trees scab to cream
and grey trees strip bright salmon, with loden patches.

Demo

No. Not from me. Never.
Not a step in your march,
not a vowel in your unison,
bray that shifts to bay.

Banners sailing a street river,
power in advance of a vote,
go choke on these quatrain tablets.
I grant you no claim ever,

not if you pushed the Christ Child
as President of Rock Candy Mountain
or yowled for the found Elixir
would your caste expectations snare me.

Superhuman with accusation,
you would conscript me to a world
of people spat on, people hiding
ahead of oncoming poetry.

Whatever class is your screen
I'm from several lower.
To your rigged fashions, I'm pariah.
Nothing a mob does is clean,

not at first, not when slowed to a media,
not when police. The first demos I saw,
before placards, were against me,
alone, for two years, with chants,

every day, with half-conciliatory
needling in between, and aloof
moral cowardice holding skirts away.
I learned your world order then.

Deaf Language

Two women were characters, continually
rewriting themselves, in turn, with their hands
mostly, but with face and torso too
and very fast, in brushwork like the gestures
above a busy street in Shanghai.

The Head-Spider

Where I lived once, a roller coaster's range
of timber hills peaked just by our backyard cliff
and cars undulated scream-driven round its seismograph
and climbed up to us with an indrawn gasp of girls.

Smiles and yelling could be exchanged as they crested
then they'd pitch over, straining back in a shriek
that volleyed as the cars were snatched from sight
in the abyss, and were soon back. Weekdays they rested,

and I rested all days. There was a spider in my head
I'd long stay unaware of. If you're raped you mostly know
but I'd been cursed, and refused to notice or believe it.
Aloof in a Push squat, I thought I was moral, or dead.

Misrule was strict there, and the Pill of the day only ever
went into one mouth, not mine, and foamed a Santa-beard.
I was resented for chastity, and slept on an overcoat.
Once Carol from upstairs came to me in bra and kindness

and the spider secreted by girls' derision-rites to spare
women from me had to numb me to a crazed politeness.
Squeals rode the edge of the thrill building. Cartoonist Mercier
drew springs under Sydney. Push lovers were untrue on principle.

It's all architecture over there now. A new roller coaster
flies its ups and downs in wealth's face like an affront.
I've written a new body that only needs a reader's touch.
If love is cursed in us, then when God exists, we don't.

Dreambabwe

Streaming, a hippo surfaces
like the head of someone
lifting, with still entranced eyes,
from a lake of stanzas.

Amanda's Painting

In the painting, I'm seated in a shield,
coming home in it up a shadowy river.
It is a small metal boat lined in eggshell
and my hands grip the gunwale rims. I'm
a composite bow, tensioning the whole boat,
steering it with my gaze. No oars, no engine,
no sails. I'm propelling the little craft with speech.
The faded rings around my loose bulk shirt
are of five lines each, a musical lineation
and the shirt is apple-red, soaking in salt birth-sheen
more liquid than the river. My cap is a teal mask
pushed back so far that I can pretend it is headgear.
In the middle of the river are cobweb cassowary trees
of the South Pacific, and on the far shore rise
dark hills of the temperate zone. To these, at this
moment in the painting's growth, my course is slant
but my eye is on them. To relax, to speak European.

One Kneeling, One Looking Down

Half-buried timbers chained corduroy
lead out into the sand
which bare feet wincing Crutch and Crotch
spurn for the summer surf's embroidery
and insects stay up on the land.

A storm engrossing half the sky
in broccoli and seething drab
and standing on one foot over the country
burrs like a lit torch. Lightning
turns air to elixir at every grab

but the ocean sky is untroubled blue
everywhere. Its storm rolls below:
sand clouds raining on sacred country
drowned a hundred lifetimes under sea.
In the ruins of a hill, channels flow,

and people, like a scant palisade
driven in the surf, jump or sway
or drag its white netting to the tide line
where a big man lies with his limbs splayed,
fingers and toes and a forehead-shine

as if he'd fallen off the flag.
Only two women seem aware of him.
One says *But this frees us. I'd be a fool —*
Say it with me, says the other. *For him to revive*
we must both say it. Say Be alive. —

But it was our own friends who got
him with a brave shot, a clever shot. —
Those are our equals: we scorn them
for being no more than ourselves.
Say it with me. Say Be alive. —

Elder sister, it is impossible. —
Life was once impossible. And flight. And speech.
It was impossible to visit the moon.
The impossible's our summoning dimension.
Say it with me. Say Be alive again. —

The younger wavers. She won't leave
nor stop being furious. The sea's vast
catchment of light sends ashore a roughcast
that melts off every swimmer who can stand.
Glaring through slits, the storm moves inland.

The younger sister, wavering, shouts *Stay dead!*
She knows how impossibility
is the only door that opens.
She pities his fall, leg under one knee
but her power is his death, and can't be dignified.

The Margin of Difference

One and one make two,
the literalist said.
So far they've made five billion,
said the lateralist, or ten
times that, if you count the dead.

A Reticence

After a silver summer
of downpour, cement-powder autumn
set in its bag. Lawns turned crunchy
but the time tap kept dribbling away.

The paddocks were void as that evening
in early childhood when the sun
was rising in the west,
round and brimming as the factory furnace door,

as I woke up after sickness.
Then it was explained to me
that I'd slept through from morning
and I sobbed because I'd missed that day,

my entire lovely day.
Without you, it might have been a prophecy.

The Harleys

Blats booted to blatant
dubbin the avenue dire
with rubbings of Sveinn Forkbeard
leading a black squall of Harleys
with Moe Snow-Whitebeard and

Possum Brushbeard and their ladies
and, sphincter-lipped, gunning,
massed leather muscle on a run,
on a roll, Santas from Hell
like a whole shoal leaning

wide-wristed, their tautness stable
in fluency, fast streetscape dwindling,
all riding astride, on the outside
of sleek grunt vehicles, woman-clung,
forty years on from Marlon.

Aurora Prone

The lemon sunlight poured out far between things
inhabits a coolness. Mosquitoes have subsided,
flies are for later heat.
Every tree's an auburn giant with a dazzled face
and the back of its head to an infinite dusk road.
Twilights broaden away from our feet too
as rabbits bounce home up defiles in the grass.
Everything widens with distance, in this perspective.
The dog's paws, trotting, rotate his end of infinity
and dam water feels a shiver few willow drapes share.
Bright leaks through their wigwam re-purple the skinny beans
then rapidly the light tops treetops and is shortened
into a day. Everywhere stands pat beside its shadow
for the great bald radiance never seen in dreams.

The Instrument

Who reads poetry? Not our intellectuals;
they want to control it. Not lovers, not the combative,
not examinees. They too skim it for bouquets
and magic trump cards. Not poor schoolkids
furtively farting as they get immunized against it.

Poetry is read by the lovers of poetry
and heard by some more they coax to the café
or the district library for a bifocal reading.
Lovers of poetry may total a million people
on the whole planet. Fewer than the players of *skat*.

What gives them delight is a never-murderous skim
distilled, to verse mainly, and suspended in rapt
calm on the surface of paper. The rest of poetry
to which this was once integral still rules
the continents, as it always did. But on condition now

that its true name is never spoken: constructs, feral poetry,
the opposite but also the secret of the rational.
And who reads that? Ah, the lovers, the schoolkids,
debaters, generals, crime-lords, everybody reads it:
Porsche, lift-off, Gaia, Cool, patriarchy.

Among the feral stanzas are many that demand your flesh
to embody themselves. Only completed art
free of obedience to its time can pirouette you
through and athwart the larger poems you are in.
Being outside all poetry is an unreachable void.

Why write poetry? For the weird unemployment.
For the painless headaches, that must be tapped to strike
down along your writing arm at the accumulated moment.
For the adjustments after, aligning facets in a verb
before the trance leaves you. For working always beyond

your own intelligence. For not needing to rise
and betray the poor to do it. For a non-devouring fame.
Little in politics resembles it: perhaps
the Australian colonists' re-inventing of the snide
far-adopted secret ballot, in which deflation could hide

and, as a welfare bringer, shame the mass-grave Revolutions,
so axe-edged, so lictor-y.
Was that moral cowardice's one shining world victory?
Breathing in dream-rhythm when awake and far from bed
evinces the gift. Being tragic with a book on your head.

Music to Me Is Like Days

        Once played to attentive faces
        music has broken its frame
        its bodice of always-weak laces
        the entirely promiscuous art
        pours out in public spaces

accompanying everything, the selections
of sex and war, the rejections.
To jeans-wearers in zipped sporrans
it transmits an ideal body
continuously as theirs age. Warrens
of plastic tiles and mesh throats
dispense this aural money
this sleek accountancy of notes
deep feeling adrift from its feelers
thought that means everything at once
like a shrugging of cream shoulders
like paintings hung on park mesh
sonore doom soneer illy chesh!
they lost the off switch in my lifetime
the world reverberates with Muzak
and Prozac. As it doesn't with poe-zac
(I did meet a Miss Universe named Verstak).
Music to me is like days
I rarely catch who composed them
if one's sublime I think God
my life-signs suspend. I nod
it's like both Stilton and cure
from one harpsichord-hum:
penicillium —
then I miss the Köchel number.
I scarcely know whose performance
of a limpid autumn noon is superior
I gather timbre outranks rhumba.
I often can't tell days apart
they are the consumers, not me
in my head collectables decay
I've half-heard every piece of music
the glorious big one with voice
the gleaming instrumental one, so choice
the hypnotic one like weed-smoke at a party
and the muscular one out of farty
cars that goes Whudda Whudda
Whudda like the compound oil heart
of a warrior not of this planet.

A Deployment of Fashion

In Australia, a lone woman
is being crucified by the Press
at any given moment.

With no unedited right
of reply, she is cast out
into Aboriginal space.

It's always for a defect in weeping:
she hasn't wept on cue
or she won't weep correctly.

There's a moment when the sharks are
still butting her, testing her protection,
when the Labor Party, or influence,

can still save her. Not the Church,
not other parties. Even at that stage
few men can rescue her.

Then she goes down, overwhelmed
in the feasting grins of pressmen,
and Press women who've moved

from being owned by men
to being owned by fashion,
these are more deeply merciless.

She is rogue property,
she must be taught her weeping.
It is done for the millions.

Sometimes the millions join in
with jokes: how to get a baby
in the Northern Territory? Just stick

your finger down a dingo's throat.
Most times, though, the millions
stay money, and the jokes

are snobbish media jokes:
Chemidenko. The Oxleymoron.
Spittle, like the flies on Black Mary.

After the feeding frenzy
sometimes a ruefully balanced last lick
precedes the next selection.

To Me You'll Always Be Spat

Baby oyster, little grip,
settling into your pinch of shape
on a flooded timber rack:

little living gravel
I'm the human you need,
one who won't eat you,

not with much relish, even
when you're maturely underexercised
inside your knuckle sandwich.

Bloodless sheep's eye, never
appear in a bottle. Always bring
ice, lemon and your wonky tub.

You have other, non-food powers:
your estuaries are kept clean as crystal,
you eat through your jacuzzi,

you make even the non-sexy
think of a reliable wet
machine of pleasure,

truly inattentive students
of French hope they heard right,
that you chant in the arbours.

Commandant-of-convicts Wallis
who got the Wallis name unfairly
hated, had you burnt alive

in millions to make mortar.
May you now dance in the streets
and support a gross of towns!

The Disorderly

We asked How old will you be
in the year Two Thousand?
Sixty two. Sixty. Fifty nine.

Unimaginable. We started running
to shin over the sliprails
of a wire fence. You're last! —

It's all right: I'll be first in Heaven!
and we jogged on to school
past a yellow-flowering guinea vine.

Cattle stood propped on the mountain.
We caught a day-blind glider possum
and took him to school. Only later

at the shoe-wearing edge of our world
did we meet kids who thought everything
ridiculous. They found us incredible.

Cream-handed men in their towns
never screamed Christ-to-Jesus! at the hills
with diabetes breath, nor talked fight

or Scotch poetry in scared timber rooms.
Such fighters had lost, we realised
but we had them to love

or else we'd be mongrels.
This saved our souls later on,
sometimes, crossing the cousinless

detective levels of the world
to the fat-free denim culture,
that country of the Attitudes.

A Postcard

A mirrory tar-top road across
a wide plain. Drizzling sky.
A bike is parked at a large book
turned down tent-fashion on the verge.
One emerging says *I read such crazy*
things in this book. 'Every bird
has stone false teeth and enters
the world in its coffin.' That's in there.

The Internationale

Baron Samedi, leaving the House of Lords,
shrugs on his shoulders and agrees to come.
Have you observed, he asks, *dat a tarantula*
is built like, but nimbler than, a Rugby scrum?

The Manche blows East like a billion tabloid pages,
annoying the Baron: *Sheer prose, dese Narrow Seas!*
but a cohort of Lundys leaps out of Leemavaddy
on an intricate tuning of spring steel in their knees.

Mardi, now svelte, hoists up a horizontal ballad
and ascends its couplets because the fire's at the top
but Macready with a wheedle of a reedy pitch-pipe conjures
the cobra whose head will fit his wet eye-socket. Pop!

Jeu d'Esprit and Jeu de Paume grace our company
and the Countess von Dredy informs us with some pain
that in Gold-Orange-Land is now the sour gherkin season.
She'd rather complete a Seminar than a Semaine.

Yall need some time on the low horse! Mardi cries
as they all skip around us with Sha-na-na and Boom!
Our energy shorten your lease of joy, cries the Baron.
But having summoned we, do you wish we trudge in gloom?

Oasis City

Rose-red city in the angles of a cut-up
green anthology: grape stanzas, citrus strophes,
I like your dirt cliffs and chimney-broom palm trees,

your pipe dream under dust, in its heads of pressure.
I enjoy your landscape blown from the Pleistocene
and roofed in stick forests of tarmacadam blue.

Your river waltzed round thousands of loops to you
and never guessed. Now it's locked in a Grand Canal,
aerated with paddlewheels, feeder of kicking sprays,

its willows placid as geese outspread over young
or banner-streamed under flood. Hey, rose-red city
of the tragic fountain, of the expensive brink,

of crescent clubs, of flags basil-white-and-tomato,
I love how you were invented and turned on:
the city as equipment, unpacking its intersections.

City dreamed wrongly true in Puglia and Antakya
with your unemployed orange-trunks globalised out of the ground,
I delight in the mountains your flat scrub calls to mind

and how you'd stack up if decanted over steep relief.
I praise your camel-train skies and tanglefoot red-gums
and how you mine water, speed it to chrome lace and slow it

to culture's ingredients. How you learn your tolerance
on hideous pans far out, by the crystals of land sweat.
Along high-speed vistas, action breaks out of you,

but sweeter are its arrivals back inside
dust-walls of evergreen, air watered with raisins and weddings,
the beer of day pickers, the crash wine of night pickers.

Towards 2000

As that monster the Twentieth Century
sheds its leathers and chains, it will cry

Automatic weapons! I shot at
millions and they died. I kept doing it,

but most not ruled by uniforms ate well
in the end. And cool replaced noble.

Nearly every black-and-white Historic figure
will look compromised by their haircut and cigarette.

And the dead will grow remoter
among words like *pillow-sham* and *boater.*

You'll admit, the old century will plead,
I developed ways to see and hear the dead.

Only briefly will TV restrain Hitler
and Napoleon from having an affair.

I changed my mind about the retarded:
I ended great for those not the full quid.

You breathers, in your rhythmic inner blush,
you dismiss me, now I'm a busted flush,

but I brought cures, mass adventures – no one's fooled.
A line called Last Century will be ruled

across all our lives, lightly at first,
even as unwiring bottles cough

their corks out, and posh aerosols burst
and glasses fill and ding, and people quaff.

You Find You Can Leave It All

Like a charging man, hit
and settling face down in the ringing,
his cause and panic obsolete,

you find you can leave it all:
your loved people, pain, achievement
dwindling upstream of this raft-fall.

Ribbed fluorescent-panels flow
over you down urgent corridors,
dismissing midday outside. Slow,

they'd resemble wet spade-widths in a pit;
you've left grief behind you, for others;
your funeral: who'll know you'd re-planned it?

God, at the end of prose,
somehow be our poem –
When forebrainy consciousness goes

wordless selves it'd barely met,
inertias of rhythm, the life habit
continue the battle for you.

If enough of those hold
you may wake up in this world,
ache-boned, tear-sponged, dripped into:

Do you know your name? 'Yes' won't do.
It's Before again, with shadow. No tunnels.
You are a trunk of prickling cells.

It's the evening of some day. But it's also
afterlife from here on, by that consent
you found in you, to going where you went.

Small Flag Above the Slaughter

Perhaps a tribal kinship,
some indigenous skinship
is equivalent to the term our neighbour saw
fit to award his amiable then-fit cuckolder,
now sick, whom he nurses:
He is my husband-in-law.

Downhill on Borrowed Skis

White mongrel I hate snow
wadded numbing mousse
grog face in a fur noose
the odd miraculous view
through glass or killing you
the only time I skied
I followed no skilled lead
but on parallel lent boards

fell straight down a hill
fell standing up by clenched will
very fast on toe-point swords
over logshapes and schist
outcrips crops it was no piste
nor had I had any drinks
wishing my ankles steel links
winging it hammer and Shazam
no stocks in afternoon mirk
every cloud-gap royally flash
like heading into a car crash
ayyy the pain! the paperwork!
my hands I didn't flail them
though neither left nor right
neither schuss nor slalom
my splitting splay twinned sled
pumping straining to spread
to a biplane wreck of snapped ligaments
all hell played with locked joints
but still I skidded down erect
in my long spill of grist
blinded hawk on a wrist
entirely unschooled unchecked
the worst going on not and not
happening no sprawl no bone-shot
till I stood on the flat
being unlatched and exclaimed at.

The Holy Show

I was a toddler, wet-combed
with my pants buttoned to my shirt
and there were pink and green lights, pretty
in the day, a Christmas-tree party
up the back of the village store.

I ran towards it, but big sad people
stepped out. They said over me *It's just, like,*
for local kiddies and *but let him join in*;
the kiddies looked frightened
and my parents, caught off guard

one beat behind me, grabbed me up
in the great shame of our poverty
that they talked about to upset themselves.
They were blushing and smiling, cursing me
in low voices *Little bugger bad boy!*

for thinking happy Christmas undivided,
whereas it's all owned, to buy in parcels
and have at home; for still not knowing
you don't make a holy show of your family;
outside it, there's only parry and front.

Once away, they angrily softened to
me squalling, because I was their kiddie
and had been right about the holy show
that models how the world should be
and could be, shared, glittering in near focus

right out to the Sex frontier.

A Riddle

The tall Wood twins
grip each other everywhere:
'It's all right, we're only
standing in for Lady Stair.' *

* Answer: a ladder

Sound Bites

Attended by thousands, the Sun is opening

★

it's a body-prayer, a shower: you're
in touch all over, renewing, enfolded in a wing –

★

My sorrow, only ninety-five thousand
welcomes left in Scots Gaeldom now.

★

Poor cultures can afford poetry, wealthy cultures can't.

★

Sex is the ever-appeased class
system that defeats Utopias . . .

★

but I bask in the pink that you're in (Repeat)

★

one day, as two continents are dividing
the whole length of a river turns salt.

★

What's sketched at light speed
thunder must track, bumbling, for miles

★

If love shows you its terrible face
before its beautiful face, you'll be punished.

★

People watching with their mouths
an increasing sky-birth of meteors

★

Y chromosomes of history, apologise to your Xes!

★

In the Costume of Andalusia

Traditional costume puts you
anywhere in its span:
was it in the eighteenth
or the twentieth century
you were photographed, in colour,
at noonday in Seville?

Strolling with your sister
or your schoolfellow, perhaps,
and wearing for your paseo
the sash of a horsewoman,
the cropped black coatee
and the levelled flat hat.

That day was your perfection,
your tan face unwrinkled
as the rain-coloured skin
of the tiny pearls that buttoned
your ears and white collar.

You were photographed by a man,
a personable foreigner.
The total attention
in your olive eyes,
the stilled line of your mouth
all equally reveal it.

The windows of your perfectly
vertical nose inhale man
but you evince none
of the arts of cliché.
Your gaze photographs
the effect of his gaze and yours.

If you had a name, we might
imagine you strolling on
into all your private pictures,
the Sierra, the Range Rover,
into time's minute razors.

Here, where you still are
as you were then, briefly being
the temper of a people,
you don't know when you're kissed

or when your burnished horse
was brought, block by block,
shuddering happily in the sun.

Autumn Cello

Driving up to visit April
who lives on the Tableland
we were sorry for russet beef cattle
deciduous on pasture hills.

We'd had to shower off summer
to climb to the Tableland
where April would be breezily
scuffing her yellow shoes.

As we crossed the caramel river
that is walled in nettle trees
and drove up through black rainforest
the moon was in our mind

it being the dark of the moon
all day, as we went up to April,
the fat moon who saw it is children
who bring death into the world

and was exiled to the sky for it
before there was any April
to plant elm trees, or touch
amber glasses with a spoon.

Next night, the moon would rise
asleep in his brilliant rim
of cradle above bared trees
and April, having forgotten

she was once herself a moon
would feed cognac–coloured rosin
to her cello bow, and read us
story-feeling without the stories

and straight depth with no sides,
all from her tilted quatrain
of strings with its blunt prong
in her Wilton rug on the Tableland.

The New Hieroglyphics

In the World language, sometimes called
Airport Road, a thinks balloon with a gondola
slung under it is a symbol for *speculation*.

Thumbs down to ear and tongue:
World can be written and read, even painted
but not spoken. People use their own words.

Latin letters are in it for names, for e.g.
OK and H_2SO_4, for musical notes,
but mostly it's diagrams: skirt-figure, trousered figure

have escaped their toilet doors. I (that is, *saya,
ego, watashi wa*) am two eyes without pupils;
those aren't seen when you look out through them.

You has both pupils, *we* has one, and one blank.
Good is thumbs up, thumb and finger zipping lips
is *confidential. Evil* is three-cornered snake eyes.

The effort is always to make the symbols obvious:
the bolt of *electricity*, winged stethoscope of course
for *flying doctor*. Pram under fire? *Soviet film industry*.

Pictographs also shouldn't be too culture-bound:
a heart circled and crossed out surely isn't.
For red, betel spit lost out to ace of diamonds.

Black is the ace of spades. The king of spades
reads *Union boss*, the two is *feeble effort*.
If is the shorthand Libra sign, the scales.

Spare literal pictures render most nouns and verbs
and computers can draw them faster than Pharaoh's scribes.
A bordello prospectus is as explicit as the action,

but everywhere there's sunflower talk, i.e.
metaphor, as we've seen. A figure riding a skyhook
bearing food in one hand is the pictograph for *grace*,

two animals in a book read *Nature*, two books
inside an animal, *instinct*. Rice in bowl with chopsticks
denotes *food*. Figure 1 lying prone equals *other*.

Most emotions are mini-faces, and the speech
balloon is ubiquitous. A bull inside one is dialect
for placards inside one. Sun and moon together

inside one is *poetry*. Sun and moon over palette,
over shoes etc. are all art forms – but above
a cracked heart and champagne glass? Riddle that

and you're starting to think in World, whose grammar
is Chinese-terse and fluid. Who needs the square-
equals-diamond book, the *dictionary*, to know figures

led by strings to their genitals mean *fashion*?
just as a skirt beneath a circle means *demure*
or a similar circle shouldering two arrows is *macho*.

All peoples are at times cat in water with this language
but it does promote international bird on shoulder.
This foretaste now lays its knife and fork parallel.

The Annals of Sheer

Like a crack across a windscreen
this Alpine sheep track winds
around buttress cliffs of sheer
no guard rail anywhere
like cobweb round a coat
it threads a bare rock world
too steep for soil to cling,
stark as poor people's need.

High plateau pasture must be great
and coming this way to it
or from it must save days
for men to have inched across
traverses, sometime since the ice age,
and then with knock and hammer
pitching reminders over-side
wedged a pavement two sheep wide.

In the international sign-code
this would be my pictograph for
cold horror, but generations

have led their flocks down and up
this flow-pipe where any spurt
or check in deliberate walking
could bring overspill and barrelling
far down, to puffs of smash, to ruin

which these men have had
the calm skills, on re-frozen
mist footing, to prevent
since before hammers hit iron.

Ernest Hemingway and the Latest Quake

In fact the Earth never stops moving.

Northbound in our millimetric shoving
we heap rainy Papua ahead of us
with tremor and fumarole and shear
but: no life without this under-ruckus.

The armoured shell of Venus doesn't move.
She is trapped in her static of hell.
The heat of her inner weight feeds enormous
volcanoes in that gold atmosphere

which her steam oceans boil above.
Venus has never known love:
that was a European error.
Heat that would prevent us gets expressed

as continent-tiles being stressed and rifted.
These make Earth the planet for lovers.
If coral edging under icy covers
or, too evolutionary slow

for human histories to observe it, a low
coastline faulting up to be a tree-line
blur landscape in rare jolts of travel
that squash collapsing masonry with blood

then frantic thousands pay for all of us.

The Images Alone

Scarlet as the cloth draped over a sword,
white as steaming rice, blue as leschenaultia,
old curried towns, the frog in its green human skin;
a ploughman walking his furrow as if in irons, but
as at a whoop of young men running loose
in brick passages, there occurred the thought
like instant stitches all through crumpled silk:

as if he'd had to leap to catch the bullet.

A stench like hands out of the ground.
The willows had like beads in their hair, and
Peenemünde, grunted the dentist's drill, Peenemünde!
Fowls went on typing on every corn key, green
kept crowding the pinks of peach trees into the sky
but used speech balloons were tacky in the river
and waterbirds had liftoff as at a repeal of gravity.

Rooms of the Sketch-Garden

for Peter and Christine Alexander

Women made the gardens, in my world,
cottage style full-sun fanfares
netting-fenced, of tablecloth colours.

Shade is what I first tried to grow
one fence in from jealous pasture,
shade, which cattle rogueing into

or let into, could devour
and not hurt much. Shelter from glare
it rests their big eyes, and rests in them.

A graphite-toned background of air
it features red, focusses yellow.
Blue diffusing through it rings the firebell.

Shade makes colours loom and be thoughtful.
It has the afterlife atmosphere
but also the philosophic stone cool.

It is both day and night civilised,
the colour of reading, the tone
of inside, and of inside the mind.

I could call these four acres Hanlin
for the Chinese things they have nourished,
loquat, elm, mulberry, the hard pear

er ben lai. But other names would fit: Klagenfurt,
Moaner's Crossing, for the many things that die,
for worn-out farm soil, for the fruit fly.

Cloud shadows walking our pencilled roof
in summer sound like a feasting chook
or Kukukuku on about duk-duk

and this sketch garden's a retina for chance:
for floodwaters backing into the lower
parterres like lorryloads of mercury

at night, or level sepia by day,
for the twenty-three sorts of native vines
along the gully; for the heron-brought

igniting propane-blue waterlily,
for the white poplars' underworld advance
on the whole earth, out of my ignorance.

Tall Australians stand east of the house
and well north. The garden's not nationalist:
Australians burn, on winds from the west.

No birds that skim-drink, or bow
or flower in our spaces are owned now.
Jojo burrs make me skid my feet on lawn

being wary of long grass, like any bushman.
Begged and scavenged plants survived dry spells
best, back when I'd to garden in absentia:

Dad wouldn't grow flowers, or water ornamentals.
He mounded for the Iroquois three sisters,
corn beans and squash. And melons, and tomatoes.

Those years we'd plant our live Christmas tree
in January when it shed its brittle bells
and the drought sun bore down like dementia.

Now bloom-beds displace fox-ripped rooster plumes
in from paddocks, in our cattle-policed laager;
trampled weeds make wharves for the indigo waterhen.

The Tin Clothes

This is the big arrival.
The zipper of your luggage
growls *valise* round three sides
and you lift out the tin clothes.

Judged Worth Evacuating

Vertical war, north of my early childhood:

in pouring high forest, men labour,
deadly furniture in hand, on mud footholds.

They eye a youth strapped between shafts
and blanched with agony, being tenderly
levered down past them by Papuans.

A hammer of impatiens flowers got him.

The Moon Man

Shadowy kangaroos moved off
as we drove into the top paddock
coming home from a wedding
under a midnightish curd sky

then his full face cleared:
Moon man, the first birth ever
who still massages his mother
and sends her light, for his having

been born fully grown.
His brilliance is in our blood.
Had Earth fully healed from that labour
no small births could have happened.

Succour

Refugees, derelicts – but why classify
people in the wreck of their terms?
These wear mixed and accidental clothing
and are seated at long tables in rows.

It's like a school, and the lesson
has moved now from papers to round
volumes of steaming food
which they seem to treat like knowledge,

re-learning it slowly, copying it
into themselves with hesitant spoons.

Predawn in Health

The stars are filtering through a tree
outside in the moon's silent era.

Reality is moving layer over layer
like crystal spheres now called laws.

The future is right behind your head;
just over all horizons is the past.

The soul sits looking at its offer.

Touchdown

The great airliner has been filled
all night with a huge sibilance
which would rhyme with FORTH
but now it banks, lets sunrise
in in freak lemon Kliegs,
eases down like a brushstroke
onto swift cement, and throws out
its hurricane of air anchors.
Soon we'll all be standing
encumbered and forbidding in the aisles
till the heads of those farthest forward
start rocking side to side, leaving,
and that will spread back:
we'll all start swaying along as
people do on planks but not on streets,
our heads tick-tocking with times
that are wrong everywhere.

The Cut-Out

In the shed it's bumped verticals,
tin and planking the colour of rain.

The sheep left their cloud inside
and two men lie wringing wet.

One man owns the flock, but neither
expects to wear the suitings.

The indoor storm of their work
earns a bit more survival, near home,

and each shearing-sling is a whale's
joined jawbones, dangling from a spring.

Visitor

He knocks at the door
and listens to his heart approaching.

Clothing as Dwelling as Shouldered Boat

Propped sheets of bark converging
over skin-oils and a winter fire,
stitched hides of a furry rug-cloak
with their naked backs to the weather,
clothing as dwelling as shouldered boat
beetle-backed, with bending ridgelines,
all this, resurrected and gigantic:
the Opera House,
Sydney's Aboriginal building.

Starry Night

In the late Nineteenth century
one is out painting landscapes
with spiralling sky
and helicopter lights approaching.

The Kettle's Bubble-Making Floor

Who remembers the bitter
smell of smoke still in the house
the sunny next afternoon?
So recently smoke was everyday.
Who remembers the woolly
pink inside a burning peat?

The taste of tank water boiled
in blanched, black-shelled cast iron?
The pucker of water heated with
ashy stones in a wooden dish?

Big Bang

If everything is receding
from everything, we're only
seeing the backs of the stars.

Worker Knowledge

The very slight S of an adze handle
or broadaxe handle are cut off square.
When adzes stopped licking timber ships
they were stubbed to scrape rabbit-trap setts.

But the worker's end of a felling axe
where the tapering upsweep levels down
to bulge, is cut slant, to the shape
of a thoroughbred's hoof pawing the ground.

Jellyfish

Globe globe globe globe
soft glass bowls upside down
over serves of nutty udder and teats
under the surface of the sun.

The Great Cuisine Cleaver Dance Sonnet

Juice-wet black steel
rectangle with square bite
dock pork slice slice
candy pork mouth size
heel-and-toe work walk
thru greens wad widths
bloc duck bisect bone
facet glaze nick snake
slit wriggle take gallbladder
whop garlic shave lily-root
wham! clay chicken-crust
hiss wok plug flare
circling soy cringing prawn
blade amassing sideways mince.

Creole Exam

How old were you when you first
lived in a weatherproof house?

Hoon Hoon

Hoon, hoon, that blowfly croon:
first a pimp and then a goon.
Sound of a prop plane crossing the moon.
The crack of noon from a can of beer
and a Viking is nothing but a rune hoon.

A Countryman

On the long flats north of the river
an elder in a leather jacket
is hitchhiking to his daughter's funeral.

The End of Symbol

From a cinder in the far blue
a wedgetail eagle used to magnify
down into arrival, into belief,
matching speeds with a boy as he
rode his bike through suburban Melbourne,
then it would fold double and alight
on his handlebars, its inarguable expression
never ruffled, but its flickknife pinions
dilating around curves, and it would
chicken-peep near inaudibly when he
caressed it beneath the flames of its neck.

Reclaim the Sites

We are spared the Avenues of Liberation
and the water-cannoned Fifths of May
but I tire of cities clogged with salutes
to other cities: York, Liverpool, Oxford Streets
and memorial royalty: Elizabeth,
Albert, William, unnumbered George.
Give me Sallie Huckstepp Road, ahead of
sepia Sussex, or Argyle, or Yankee numbering
– and why not a whole metropolis
street-signed for its own life and ours:
Childsplay Park and First Bra Avenue,
Unsecured Loan, the Boulevard Kiss,
Radar Strip, Bread-Fragrance Corner,
Fumbletrouser, Delight Bridge, Timeless Square?

The Bellwether Brush

As the painter Sali Herman discerns
and captures the iron-lace character
of what are still called slums then
he's unaware the bright haze his brush
confers is called Billions;
he delightedly thinks Beauty, Truth,
but fashion turns its head, and starts
walking clap-clap in the footsteps,
clap-clap, of his easel,
walking in twos, as coppers used to,
till the salt of the earth accept
hot offers for their bijou homes.

In a Time of Cuisine

A fact the gourmet
euphemism can't silence:
vegetarians eat sex,
carnivores eat violence.

Uplands

Across silvering cobble
                    into white-ant stump country.
Hills lie where they fell;
                    boulders sultana their steeps.

Smoke wanders up from a couple of far places.

Crested trees pour their shade
                    to one side on the ground.

Unplugging their weight,
                    kangaroos hoist up, and bounce.

A hill's front becoming its back
                    takes the sun all day.

Forest up some slopes,
                    thin enough to see grass under.

Getting well out now
                    back into the high country.

Mountains pregnant with hills in a white skim sky.

The Pay for Fosterage

The carpenter could have stayed
hunched over, at work on his chagrin,
left everything to the hush-ups
and stone-evadings of women.
He could have escaped the thousands
of years of speculation. The horns.
But all that weakness was behind him.
The courteous presence had spoken
unearthly sense to its equal,
himself. As he would be from now
on into the world to come.

A Study of the Nude

Someone naked with you
will rarely be a nude.
A nude is never with just one.

205

Nude looks back at everyone
or no one. Aubergine or bluish rose,
a nude is a generalization.

Someone has given their name
and face to be face all over,
to be the face of something

that isn't for caressing
except with the mind's hand.
Nude is the full dress of undressing.

Iguassu

Shallow at brinks
with pouring tussocks
a bolt of live tan water
is continuously tugged
off miles of table
by thunderous white claws.

Pietà Once Attributed to Cosme Tura

This is the nadir of the story.

His mother's hairpiece, her *sheitel,*
is torn away, her own cropped hair looks burnt.
She had said the first Mass
and made Godhead a fact
which his strangeness had kept proving,
but what of that is still true
now, with his limp weight at her knee?
Her arms open, and withdraw,
and come back. That first Eucharist
she could have been stoned to death for
is still alive in her body.

The Knockdown Question

Why does God not spare the innocent?

The answer to that is not in
the same world as the question
so you would shrink from me
in terror if I could answer it.

The Insiders

What's in who for you?
Who's in you for himself?

Pop Music

Empty as a country town street
after five. Two or three crisp
high-heel walkers, and a pair
of little girls in a station wagon,
one bunging a pop bottle *boinc*
against her head and *bocc*
against the wagon. The other blows
music into hers: *Doe roe to hoe soon
but no throe for woe yet, moon!*

The Body in Physics

The air has sides, in a house.
Birds, whacked from colliding, embrace
its sheer with umbrella-rib skiddings.
They gape silent death-cries when closed
in converging hands, or snatched out
of such parts of their theory as still fly.
Carried outside, they pause a beat
and drop upwards, into gravity that once more
blows as well as sucks. Fliers' gravity.

Fruit Bat Colony by Day

High above its gloom
this forest is all hung
with head-down ginger bats
like big leather bees.
In sun to stay drowsy
daylong in slow dangle
chi-chi as monkeys
they blow on sad tin horns,
glide, nurture babies, sleep,
waiting for their real lives.

The Climax of Factory Farming

Farm gates were sealed with tape;
people couldn't stop shaking their heads.
Out on the fells and low fields
in twilight, it was the Satanic mills
come again: the farm beasts of Britain
being burnt inside walls of their feed.

The Poisons of Right and Left

You are what you have got
and: to love, you have to hate.
Two ideas that have killed and maimed
holocausts and myriads.

The Top Alcohol Contender

An aircraft-engined kewpie doll
in chrome, with vast fat tyres,
stinks hotly of injection and rubdown
and little wheels splay at the far
end of its blood-red stick –
how else should it look,
the top alcohol contender?

Apsley Falls

Abounding white water
details each stratum
on basalt stratum
down hundreds and hundreds
like bands of washed linen,
this mummy standing up
the height of its mountain
in an ink-wet corridor.

To One Outside the Culture

Still ask me about adult stuff
when you want. But remember that day
in Madame Tussaud's basement
when all the grownups looked careful
and some young ones had to smirk?

You were right to cry out in horror
at the cut-off heads there
and the rusty dried trickles
shocked out of their eyes and ears.

Portrait of a Felspar-Coloured Cat

Plaintive, she named herself Min
in the reaching-down world.

Her texture manages itself;
her comet tail is Abyssinian.

All her intelligence
is elegance.

Never would soil she flicked up
persist in her belly fur.

At University

Puritans reckoned the cadavers
in Anatomy were drunks off the street;
idealists said they were benefactors
who had willed their bodies to science,

but the averted manila-coloured
people on the tables had pinned-back
graves excavated in them
around which they lay scattered in the end
as if exhumed from themselves.

The Young Fox

I drove up to a young fox
on the disused highway.
It didn't scare, but watched me
roll up to it along the asphalt.
I got out. Any poultry it would kill
wouldn't now be mine. No feud between us.

It watched quizzically, then bounded
away with an unmistakeable headshake
that says *Play with me!*
and stopped, waiting. I remember
how sharply perfumed the leaves were
that lay on the pavement in that world.

Experience

I heard a cat bark like a fox
because the car's larger purr
didn't soothe her, locked in a cat-box
and the hitchhiker said *We keep a snake*
to eat our rats! For heaven's sake.
I've heard a snake hiss like a man
I saw a goose sail like a bark
I heard a man wank like a goose.

The Barcaldine Suite

High on mountains worldwide they blow
on long wood trumpets in tones of psalm
summoning weirdness or cattle or calm
or play a wood horse with a horsehair bow
and the didgeridoo, that lowland shofar,
throttles where dancing and secrets are –

    Dance leaped from the Bang
    finding orbital speeds

    Life joined it underwater
    brought it skyward as reeds

    and half of dance air-dried
    into carolling and birds

    into drumming and howling
    and the human song, words –

Musicians mug outwards
dancing with their instruments
or stare deeply inward
communing with their instruments,
displaying the catch
or listening for the prey –

    The band vamped along
    to music pince-nez'ed to a tuba
    and this woman stood in tears.
    It was sunny Europe to her

    and a Pentecost of tones
    came to ignition over towns
    getting nubs and gists uttered
    that talk had often spattered –

Music is the great nonsense poem
written, for recital if at all,
in the old bonding lingo of cry
that we translate experience into
dilly-O Johnny Ringo bye bye
to check with the tree-nests of Home.

Music is the vast nonsense poem
our precisions float out on with emotion
to change and get poignant as they drown;
la Musique: it needs no translation.
It can back up, or send up, any Line;
it makes even the thought-police hum.

Tart angel that never lost Heaven
O waly the faraway wine
music is the great nonsense poem,
the religion no hard nose rejects,
not trapped in the medium of critics.
O harmonium the zillion-armed Om –

    Being deeply moved
    stops movement. Voice would be fur –

    The soul is open. Something
    always knew its key –

    laughter and crying at once,
    or rapt, or fainting to sleep –

    gooseflesh fades to shiver
    as the modern resumes –

I thought of ambient sounds that music has dipped up
in its silver ladle: heartbeats and hoofbeats, and trains
volleying with tipplers and Dopplers, or blue in the night,
drips in echoey spaces, wind through frightful places,
factory-crash heavy metal, the strung pluck of bows,
bells, whistles, the clinker coming at you across everything,
peaks peaks peaks of murder. And crowds, and the ocean snore.

It's a shortish list, even with the anvil and the cannon.
Has nobody scored the rippy un-tiling of a fish?
The colic in tennis courts? The blowfly race-call tune
that evokes no sex on a long flat saturday?

What about steamships, beyond the lorn siren to the barrel
and tumbledom of their nature, or the huge bulk gamelan
as hardwood logs collaborate into a keen sawmill?
Uneven steps rasping slowly, with rests, downhill?

    The weight of our weight
    the weight of our years —

I know the purist point isn't wild sound being redeemed
up into music, but what of music's own dimension
can be modulated into existence for the mind.
A body of its own for the mind, with no fixed visuals.
Without the beards and sweaters of hand-rolled wool
would work songs sound like politics? Would the symphonic,
without posh and penguin suits, still sound like a wall of money? —

The weight of our weight
the weight of our years
the said and the shed and the
stammered in tears
and always this broadcast
Otherworld at our ears —

Then, we'll be a tune
they'll put on and play
bits of and rarely
till our times pass away
and there's no one on earth
who knew us by heart.
Obsolete for all time
and that's just the start.

The Meaning of Existence

Everything except language
knows the meaning of existence.
Trees, planets, rivers, time
know nothing else. They express it
moment by moment as the universe.

Even this fool of a body
lives it in part, and would
have full dignity within it
but for the ignorant freedom
of my talking mind.

The Aboriginal Cricketer

Mid-19th century

Good-looking young man
in your Crimean shirt
with your willow shield
up, as if to face spears,

you're inside their men's Law,
one church they do obey;
they'll remember you were here.
Keep fending off their casts.

Don't come out of character.
Like you, they suspect
idiosyncrasy of witchcraft.
Above all, don't get out

too easily, and have to leave here
where all missiles are just leather
and come from one direction.
Keep it noble. Keep it light.

The Aztec Revival

Human sacrifice has come back
on another city-island
and bloodied its high stepped towers.

Few now think the blood's redeemed
by red peppers, or turkey in chocolate.
Human sacrifice comes, now always,

in default of achievement,
from minds that couldn't invent
the land-galaxies of dot painting

or new breakthrough zeroes, or jazz.

The Averted

The one whose eyes
do not meet yours
is alone at heart
and looks where the dead look
for an ally in his cause.

Post Mortem

I was upstaged in Nottingham
after reading poetry there
by what lay in the porter's room above:
ginger human skeletons. Eight of them.

Disturbed by extensions to the arts centre
and reassembled from the dozer's shove
some might have been my ancestors, Nottingham
being where my mother's people fled from

in the English Civil War.
These were older than that migration,
crusty little roundheads of sleep,
stick-bundles half burned to clay by water.

Their personhoods had gone, into the body
of that promise preached to them. What had stayed
in their bones were their diseases, the marks
of labour in a rope-furrowed shoulder blade,

their ages when they died, and what they'd eaten:
bread, bacon, beer, cheese, apples, greens,
no tomato atoms in them, no potatoeines,
no coffee yet, or tea, or aspirin

but alcoholic curds horn-spooned at a fair
and opium physic, and pease porridge.
The thought that in some cells their
programmes might persist, my far parentage,

attracted me no more than re-building
faces for them with wire and moulding.
Unsatisfied to go as a detective
to the past, I want the past live

with the body we have in the promise,
that book which opens when the story ends.
Being even a sound modern physique
is like owning an apartment in Venice.

The Hanging Gardens

High on the Gloucester road
just before it wriggles its hips
level with eagles down the gorge
into the coastal hills

there were five beige pea-chickens
sloping under the farm fence
in a nervous unison of head-tufts
up to the garden where they lived

then along the gutter and bank
adult birds, grazing in full serpent.
Their colours are too saturate and cool
to see at first with dryland eyes

trained to drab and ginger. No one here
believes in green deeply enough. In greens
so blue, so malachite. Animal cobalt too
and arrow bustles, those are unparalleled.

The wail lingers, and their cane
surrection of iridium plaques. Great spirits,
Hindoostan in the palette of New Zealand!
They don't succeed at feral.

Things rush them from dry grass.
Haggard teeth climb to them. World birds,
human birds, flown by their own volition
they led us to palaces.

Leaf Brims

A clerk looks again at a photo,
decides, puts it into a file box
which he then ties shut with string
and the truth is years away.

A Naval longboat is rowed upstream
where jellied mirrors fracture light
all over sandstone river walls
and the truth is years away.

A one-inch baby clings to glass
on the rain side of a window as
a man halts, being led from office
but the truth is years away.

Our youngest were still child-size when
starched brims of the red lotus last
nodded over this pond in a sunny breeze
and the truth was years away.

The Statistics of Good

Chaplain General (R.C.)
Archbishop Mannix of Melbourne,
he who had a bog-oak footstool
so his slipper might touch Irish soil
first, when alighting from his carriage

saved, while a titular Major General
in the Australian Army, perhaps half
the fit men of a generation
from the shrapnelled sewer landscapes
of Flanders by twice winning close
referenda against their conscription.

How many men? Half a million? Who knows?
Goodness counts *each* and *theirs.*
Politics and Death chase the numbers.

Twelve Poems

That wasn't horses: that was
rain yawning to life in the night
on metal roofs.

★

Lying back so smugly
phallic, the ampersand
in the deckchair of itself.

★

Fish head-down in a bucket
wave their helpless fan feet.

★

Spirituality?
she snorted. And poetry?
They're like yellow and gold.

★

Being rushed through the streets
at dusk, by trees and rain, the
equinoctial gales!

★

The best love poems are known
as such to the lovers alone.

★

Creek pools, grown top heavy,
are speaking silver-age verse
through their gravel beards.

★

Have a heart: salted land
is caused by human tears.

★

Tired from understanding
life, the animals approach man
to be mystified.

★

A spider walking
in circles is celebrating
the birthday of logic.

★

To win me, they told me
all my bad attitudes
but they got them wrong.

★

Filling in a form
the simple man asks his mother
Mum, what sex are we?

Travelling the British Roads

Climb out of mediaeval one-way
and roundabouts make knotted rope
of the minor British roads
but legal top speed on the rocketing
nickel motorway is a lower limit!
I do it, and lorries howl past me.

Sometimes after brown food
at a pub, I get so slow
that Highland trackways
only have one side
since they are for feet
and hoofs of pack horses
and passing is ceremony.

Nor is it plovers
which cry in the peopled glens
but General Wade's chainmen
shouting numbers for his road
not in the Gaelic scores
but in decimal English.

Universal roads return as shoal
late in the age of iron rims.
Stones in the top layer to be
no bigger than would fit in your mouth,
smiles John McAdam. *If in doubt*
test them with your lips!

Highwaymen, used to reining in
thoroughbreds along a quag of track,
suddenly hang, along new carriageways
or clink iron on needy slave-ships,
but wagon horses start surviving
seven years instead of three
at haulage between new smoke towns.

Then railways silence the white road.
A horseman rides alone between villages;
the odd gig, or phaeton;
smoke and music of the *bosh*
rising out of chestnut shade:
Gypsies, having a heyday.
Post roads, drying out, seem strange
beaches, that intersect each other.

When housemaids uncovered their hair
at windows, and a newfangled
steam roller made seersucker sounds
there were swans on the healed canal,
and with the sun came the Queen's
Horse Artillery in tight skeleton coats
to exercise their dubbined teams
watched by both fashionable sexes
in bloomer-like pedal pants.

I knew to be wary of the best dressed,
decent with the footsore,
but frontier-raffish with all
because the scripts they improvised from
were dry and arch, but quickly earnest.

From that day, and the audible
woodwind cry of peafowl, it was half
a long lifetime till jerked motors
would ripple the highroad
with their soundwaves, like a palate,
and kiss its gravel out
with round rubber lips
growling for the buckets of tar

and another life to the autobahn
nothing joins, where I race the mirror
in a fighter cockpit made posh
under flak of Guy Fawkes eve
over the cities of fumed brick.

Winter Winds

Like appliqué on nothingness
like adjectives in hype
fallen bracts of the bougain-
magenta-and-faded-villea
eddy round the lee verandah
like flowers still partying
when their dress has gone home.

The Tune on Your Mind

Asperges me hyssopo
the snatch of plainsong went,
Thou sprinklest me with hyssop
was the clerical intent,
not *Asparagus with hiccups*
and never *autistic savant.*

Asperger, mais. Asperg is me.
The coin took years to drop:

Lectures instead of chat. The want
of people skills. The need for Rules.
Never towing a line from the Ship of Fools.
The avoided eyes. Great memory.
Horror not seeming to perturb –
Hyssop can be a bitter herb.

A Dialect History of Australia

Bralgu. Kata Tjuta. Lutana.

Cape Leeuwin Abrolhos Groote Eylandt.

Botany Bay Cook Banksia Kangaroo Ground
Sydney Cove Broad Arrow Neutral Bay China Walls
Sodwalls Hungerford Cedar Party Tailem Bend
Jackadgery Loveday Darwin Kilmany. Come-by-Chance
Lower Plenty Eureka Darling Downs Dinner Plain
Telegraph Point Alice Maryfarms Diamantina
Combo Waterhole Delegate Federal Spion Kop
Hermannsburg Floreat Emu Heights. Pozieres
Monash Diggers Rest. Longreach The Gabba Hollow Tree
Perisher Police Point. Hawker Kuttabul Owens Gap
Greenslopes Repat. Red Bluff Curl Curl Charmhaven
Cracow York Kalimna Howrah. Wave Hill.
Beenleigh Yea Boort Iron Baron Long Pocket
Grange Nowhere Else Patho Tullamarine. Timor.

For an Eightieth Birthday

i.m. Lewis Deer

On a summer morning after the war
you're walking with the Belle of the Ball
both in your new pressed sports gear
over grass towards the scotching sound
of tennis balls on lined antbed
inside the netting's tall swarm.

You glance past the wartime rifle range
below the great cattle hill
that lifts your family name high
and into the gap the Japanese
soldiers never reached, there where
your years of farming will happen.

Bounce comes in your step from strung
racquets, from neighbours still young,
from unnoticed good of sun and birds
and the understandings calmly dancing
between you two, walking into the stroke-play
of gee-ups on a tournament Saturday.

Melbourne Pavement Coffee

Storeys over storeys without narrative
an estuarine vertical imperative
plugged into vast salt-pans of pavement
and higher hire over the river
ignited words pouring down live:

there an errant dog is running
nose down like a pursuit car
police car! police car! central city
and trams that look always oncoming
stop, and stand shimmering like cymbals
after the mesh! of their pair.

Here posture is better, suitings thicker
and footmen are said to survive
behind oaks up the odd gravel drive.
We saw a wall of tomato
blazer-backs striped blue-and-yellow
ranged right across their school stage
just like an inland rain painting.

We heard our grandest parliament sigh
down Bourke Street *My country, why
did you leave me, and change at Albury?*
History made here touched the world.
Now a demoted capital bleeds politics
Burnet's immune system was right wing!
down the microphone, black ice-cream cone,
down the cinecamera, New Age monocle.

Not housing, but characterful houses
lace-trimmed like picnic day blouses
reigned when beer went with cray.
Now the crayfish are Formula One
cars, flat out in raging procession –
but we're off to where the river
learns and teaches the Bay.

Black Belt in Marital Arts

Pork hock and jellyfish. Poor cock.
King Henry had a marital block.
A dog in the manager? Don't mock!
denial flows past Cairo.

A rhyme is a pun that knows where
to stop. Puns pique us with the glare
of worlds too coherent to bear
by any groan person.

Nothing moved him like her before.
It was like hymn and herbivore,
Serbs some are too acerbic for –
punning moves toward music.

The Welter

How deep is the weatherfront of time
that advances, roaring and calm
unendingly between *was* and *will be*?
A millisecond? A few hours? All secular life
worldwide, all consequences of past life
travel in it. It's weird to move ahead of,

so I went back to 1938,
the year of the Sesquicentennial,
and it was bare as a drought landscape
under a weakened sun. I found few objects,
a dessicated brougham in a slab lean-to,
a phrenological head defined in segments,

all sparse dead matter from far earlier times.
Underfoot at first were ghostly streets, but I
found my valley by its shapes. No trace of home.
My birth and my family were still travelling
in the time-front and beyond it. Mr Speed,
the last convict, who had died that year

may be travelling too, in effects of his life.
All the human figures I thought I saw
away on that country proved to be
tall old-style window tombstones. I became
aware that all the clouds there'd ever been
were up ahead, being recycled in the life-front.

Beyond flat furrows and exhausted wire
salt frosted the cobble of parched waterholes.
But tears underlie every country. Nowhere do they
discharge the past, which is the live dark matter
that flows undismissably with us, and impends
unseen over every point we reach. One day

over wing-collared futures towered the dinosaur.

A Levitation of Land

October 2002

Haze went from smoke-blue to beige
gradually, after midday.
The Inland was passing over
high up, and between the trees.
The north hills and the south hills
lost focus and faded away.

As the Inland was passing over
lungless flies quizzing road kill
got clogged with aerial plaster.
Familiar roads ended in vertical
paddocks unfenced in abstraction.
The sun was back to animating clay.

The whole ploughed fertile crescent
inside the ranges' long bow
offered up billion-tonne cargo
compound of hoofprints and debt,
stark street vistas, diesel and sweat.
This finest skim of drought particles

formed a lens, fuzzy with grind,
a shield the length of Northern Europe
and had the lift of a wing
which traffic of thermals kept amassing
over the mountains. Grist the shade
of kitchen blinds sprinkled every scene.

A dustbowl inverted in the sky
shared the coast out in bush-airfield sizes.
A surfer from the hundred-acre sea
landed on the beach's narrow squeak
and re-made his home town out of pastry.
A sense of brown snake in the air

and dogs whiffed, scanning their nosepaper.
Teenagers in the tan foreshortening
regained, for moments, their child voices,
and in double image, Vanuatu to New Zealand
an echo-Australia gathered out on the ocean
having once more scattered itself from its urn.

Through the Lattice Door

This house, in lattice to the eaves,
diagonals tacked across diagonals,

is cool as a bottle in wicker.
The sun, through stiff lozenge leaves,

prints verandahs in yellow Argyle.
Under human weight, the aged floorboards

are subtly joined, and walk with you;
French windows along them flicker.

In this former hospital's painted wards
lamplit crises have powdered to grief.

Inner walling, worn back to lead-blue,
stays moveless as the one person still

living here stands up from reading,
the one who returned here from her life,

up steps, inside the guesswork walls,
since in there love for her had persisted.

On the North Coast Line

The train coming on up the Coast
fitting like a snake into water
is fleeing the sacrificial crust
of suburbs built into fire forest.
Today, smoke towers above there.

We've winged along sills of the sea
we've traversed the Welsh and Geordie
placenames where pickaxe coughing
won coal from miners' crystal lungs.
No one aboard looks wealthy:

wives, non-drivers, Aborigines,
sun-crackled workers. The style
of country trains isn't lifestyle.
River levees round old chain-gang towns
fall away behind our run of windows.

By cuttings like hangars filled with rock
to Stroud Road, and Stratford on the Avon,
both named by Robert Dawson, who ordered
convicts hung for drowning Native children
but the Governor stopped him. God

help especially the underdogs of underdogs
and the country now is spread hide
harnessed with sparse human things
and miles ahead, dawning into mind
under its approaching cobalt-inked

Chinese scroll of drapefold mountains
waits Dawson's homesick Gloucester
where Catholics weren't allowed to live.
There people crowd out onto the platform
to blow smoke like a regiment, before windows

carry them on, as ivory phantoms
who might not quip, or sue,
between the haunches of the hills
where the pioneer Isabella Mary Kelly
(She poisons flour! Sleeps with bushrangers!

She flogs her convicts herself!)
refusing any man's protection
rode with pocket pistols. Which
on this coast, made her the Kelly
whom slander forced to bear the whole guilt,

when it was real, of European settlement.
Now her name gets misremembered:
Kelly's crossing, Kate Kelly's Crossing
and few battlers on this train
think they live in a European settlement

and on a platform down the first
subtropic river, patched velvet girls
get met by their mothers' lovers,
lawn bowlers step down clutching their nuclei
and a walking frame is hoisted yea! like swords.

The Nostril Songs

P. Ovidius Naso
when banished from Rome
remained in the city
for days on slave clothing,
for weeks in his study,
for decades in living noses –

★

Trees register the dog

and the dog receives the forest
as it trots toward the trees

then the sleeping tiger
reaches the dog en masse
before the dog reaches the tiger:

this from the Bengal forests
in the upper Kerosene age,

curry finger-lines in shock fur.

★

The woman in the scarlet tapestry
who stands up on a sprigged cushion
of land in space, is in fact
nude, as all are in the nostril-world.

What seem to be her rich gowns
are quotations from plants and animals
modulating her tucked, demure
but central olfactory heart

and her absent lover, pivoting
on his smaller salt heart
floats banner-like above her.

★

No stench is infra dog.

★

Fragrance stays measured,
stench bloats out of proportion:
even a rat-sized death,
not in contact with soil, is soon
a house-evacuating metal gas
in our sinuses; it boggles our gorge.
No saving that sofa:
give it a Viking funeral!

★

The kingdom of ghosts
has two nostril doors
like the McDonald's symbol.

You are summoned to breathe
the air of another time
that is home, that is desperate,
the tinctures, the sachets.

You yourself are a ghost.
If you were there
you are still there —

even if you're alive
out in the world of joking.

For other species, the nasal kingdom
is as enslaved and barbed
as the urine stars around all territory,

as the coke lines of autumn
snorting into a truffle-pig's head

or the nose-gaffed stallion,
still an earner, who screams rising
for the tenth time in a day.

★

Mammal self-portraits
are everywhere, rubbed on
or sprayed on in an instant.

Read by nose, they don't give
the outline shapes demanded
by that wingless bird the human;

with our beak and eyes
we perceive them as smears
or turds, or nothing at all.

Painted from inside
these portraits give the inner
truth of their subject

with no reserve or lie.
Warned or comforted or stirred
every mammal's an unfoolable

connoisseur, with its fluids
primed to judge, as it moves
through an endless exhibition.

★

Half the reason for streets,
they're to walk in the buzz
the sexes find vim in,
pheromones for the septa
of men and of women.

★

If my daddy isn't gone
and I smell his strength and care
I won't grow my secret hair
till a few years later on
on Tasmania. Down there.

★

When I was pregnant
says your sister, my nose
suddenly went acute:
I smelled which jars and cartons
were opened, rooms away,
which neighbours were in oestrus,
the approach of death in sweat.
I smelt termites in house-framing
all through a town, that mealy taint.
It all became as terrible
as completely true gossip
would be. Then it faded,
as if my baby had learned
enough, and stopped its
strange unhuman education.

★

A teaspoon upside down
in your mouth, and chopping onions
will bring no tears to your cheeks.
The spoon need not be silver.

★

Draw the cork from the stoic age
and the nose is beer and whisky.
I'll drink wine and call myself sensitive!
was a jeer. And it could be risky.

Wesleyans boiled wine for Communion;
a necked paper bag was a tramp;
one glass of sweet sherry at Christmas,
one flagon for the fringe-dwellers' camp.

You rise to wine or you sink to it
was always its Anglo bouquet.

★

When we marched against the government
it would use its dispersant gas
Skunk Hour. Wretched, lingering experience.
When we marched on the neo-feudal
top firms, they sprayed an addictive
fine powder of a thousand hip names
that was bliss in your nostrils, in your head.
Just getting more erased our other causes
and it was kept illegal, to be dear,
and you could destroy yourself to buy it
or beg with your hands through the mesh,
self-selecting, as their chemists did say.

★

Mars having come nearest our planet
the spacecraft Beagle Two went
to probe and sniff and scan it
for life's irrefutable scent,
the gas older than bowels: methane,
strong marker of digestion from the start,
life-soup-thane, amoeba-thane, tree-thane.

Sensors would screen Ares' bouquet
for paleo- or present micro-fartlets,
even one-in-a-trillion pico-partlets,
so advanced is the state of the art.
As Mars lit his match in high darkness
Beagle Two was jetting his way.

★

In the lanes of Hautgout
where foetor is rank
Gog smites and Pong strikes
black septums of iron
to keep the low down.
Ride through, nuzzle your pomander:
Don't bathe, I am come to Town:

Far ahead, soaps are rising,
bubble baths and midday soaps.
Death to Phew, taps for Hoh!
Cribs from your Cologne water.

★

Ylang ylang
elan élan
the nostril caves
that breathe stars in
and charm to Spring
the air du temps
tune wombs to sync
turn brut men on

Sir Right, so wrong —
scent, women's sense
its hunters gone
not its influence!
nose does not close
adieu sagesse

The Newcastle Rounds

Tall sails went slack, so high did Nobbys stand
so they felled him in the surf to choke on sand
and convicts naked as legs in trousers
tunnelled for coal way below the houses.

Workers got wages and the Co-op Store,
wearing bowler hats as they waltzed through the door.
They danced in pumps and they struck with banners
and they ran us up a city with spans and spanners.

When Esssington Lewiss blew through his name
steel ran in rivers, coke marched in flame.
Wharfies handled wire rope bloody with jags
and took their hands home in Gladstone bags.

Then the town break-danced on earthquake feet
and tottered on crutches down every street.
We all sniffed coke back then, for pay,
but the city came up stately when the smoke blew away.

With horses up the valley and wines flowing down
clinking their glasses as a health to the town
freighters queued off the port at all times,
from pub to art show became a social sway,
the original people got a corner of a say
and the ocean spoke to surfers in whitecap rhymes.

The House Left in English

The house has stopped its desperate travelling.
It won't fly to New Orleans, or to Hungary again,
though it counts, and swears, in Magyar.

It is left in English with its life suspended,
meals in the freezer, clothes on airy shelves,
ski badges prickling a wall chart of the Alps.

The house plays radio, its lights clock on and off
but it won't answer the phone, even in Swiss German.
Since the second recession of helped steps

the house quotes from its life and can't explain:
dress-cutter's chalk. Melbourne Cup Day 1950.
Alphorn skullcaps. Wartime soy flour, with an onion!

All earlier houses and times, in black and white
are boxed by aged children visiting to dust this one
on its leafy corner and still, for a while, in colour.

Yregami

A warm stocking caught among limbs
evokes a country road
and tufted poodles growing out
on the paddocks sway like seared trunks.

Sliced whitefish bony with wind
and very high up recall an autumn day;
arrows showering far below them at a town
speed as flights of wires.

Glazed bush ballads rhymed in concrete
pose as modern office buildings
and a sated crowd leaving a ground
after a draw feels like a stage in love.

This horse seated on a chamber pot
swinging its head and forelock,
you'd swear it was a drunk old man.

Upright Clear Across

for Kay Alden

It's like when, every year, flooding
in our river would be first to cut
the two-lane Pacific Highway.
We kids would pedal down barefoot

to the long ripple of the causeway
and wade, deep in freezing fawn energy,
ahead of windscreens slashing rain.
We were all innocent authority.

The through traffic was mostly wise
enough not to try our back roads
so we'd draw the North Coast back together,
its trips, its mercy dashes, its loads,

slow-dancing up to our navel
maybe with a whole train of followers.
Each step was a stance, with the force
coming all from one side between shores.

Every landing brought us ten bobs and silver
and a facing lot with a bag on their motor
wanting us to prove again what we
had just proved, that the causeway was there.

We could have, but never did, lose our footing
or tangle in a drowning fence
from which wire might be cut for towing –
and then bridges came, high level,
and ant-logs sailed on beneath affluence.

The Shining Slopes and Planes

Having tacked loose tin panels
of the car shed together
Peter the carpenter walks straight up
the ladder, no hands,
and buttons down lapels of the roof.

Now his light weight is on the house
overhead, and then he's back down
bearing long straps of a wiry green
Alpine grass, root-woven, fine as fur
that has grown in our metal rain gutters.

Bird-seeded, or fetched by the wind
it has had twenty years up there
being nourished on cloud-dust, on washings
of radiant iron, on nesting debris
in which pinch-sized trees had also sprouted.

Now it tangles on the ground. And the laundry
drips jowls of coloured weight
below one walking stucco stucco
up and down overlaps, to fix
the biplane houses of Australia.

The Succession

A llama stood in Hannover, with a man
collecting euros for its sustenance.
The camelid had a warm gaze. Its profound
wool was spun of the dry cloud of heaven.

My fingers ached with cold in October.
I had to fly on to Great Britain.

There the climate spared them, and Guy Fawkes
dotted on for weeks, pop, Somme and flare,

as if the wars of tabloid against Crown
were swelling up to a bitter day in Whitehall —
but battle never burst out from under the horizon.
Leaves and cock pheasants went dizzily to their fall:

the birds often stuck like eyebrows to the road.
They and grouse, shot, were four bob at the butchers
long ago when we'd wintered at Culloden.
Two and a scavenged swede, and we were fed.

Back then we weren't quite foreign, and the Dole
called on us at home. Our own country's hard welfare
made this a prodigy to us, like reverse arrest!
When the media are king, will only fear be civil?

The Offshore Island

Terra cotta of old rock undergirds
this mile of haze-green island
whitening odd edges of the sea.

It is unbrowsed by hoofed beasts
and their dung has not been on it.
Trees of the ice age have stayed rare

though no more firesticks come out
from the long smoky continent
lying a canoe-struggle to the west.

The knee-high bush is silvered canes,
bracken, unburnt grasses, bitou.
Miners came, and ate the mutton birds.

Greeks camped out there in lean times
fishing. Their Greek islands lived in town
with their families. Now it's National Park.

The world shrinks as it fills.
Outer niches revert to space, in which
to settle is soon too something.

The Hoaxist

Whatever sanctifies itself draws me.
Whether I come by bus or Net,
rage and fun are strapped around my body.

I don't kill civilians. I terrorise
experts and their elites. I drink their bubbly,
I wander among their principles

then at a pull of my cord
I implode. And laughter cascades in,
flooding those who suddenly abhor me.

The media, who are Columbine
with their prom queens and jocks,
unsheathe their public functions

and prolong the drowning frenzy.
The thought police, cavorting
and converting in equal fury.

Sometimes my cord has to be pulled
for me by others. Or I cut it off.
A buried hoax can be a career, a literature –

Ah, Koepenick! Oh, Malley! My Ossianic Celts
brought us the Romantic Era,
my Piltdowns can resurge as stars!

The Cool Green

Money just a means to our ends?
No. We are terms in its logic.
Money is an alien.

Millions eat garbage without it.
Money too can be starved
but we also die for it then,
so who is the servant?

Its weakest forms wear retro disguise:
subtly hued engraved portraits
of kings, achievers, women in the Liberty cap,
warlords who put new nations on the map –

but money is never seen nude.
Credit cards, bullion, bare numbers,
electronic, in columnar files
are only expressions of it,
and we are money's genitals.

The more invisible the money
the vaster and swifter its action,
exchanging us for shopping malls,
rewriting us as cities and style.

If I were king, how often
would I come up tails?
Only half the time
really? With all my severed heads?

Our waking dreams feature money everywhere
but in our sleeping dreams
it is strange and rare.

How did money capture life
away from poetry, ideology, religion?
It didn't want our souls.

Death from Exposure

That winter. We missed her stark face
at work. Days till she was found, under

his verandah. Even student torturers
used to go in awe. She had zero small talk.

It made no sense she had his key.
It made no sense all she could have

done. Depression exhausts the mind.
She phones, no response, she drives up

straight to his place in the mountains,
down a side road, frost all day.

You knock. What next? You can't manage
what next. Back at last, he finds her car.

She's crawled in, under, among the firewood.
Quite often the world is not round.

Me and Je Reviens

My great grand-uncle invented haute couture. Tiens,
I am related to Je Reviens!

It is the line of Worth, Grandmother's family
that excuses me from chic. It's been done for me.

When Worths from Coolongolook, Aboriginal and white,
came out of Fromelles trenches on leave from the fight

they went up to Paris and daringly located
the House of Worth. At the doors, they hesitated −

but were swept from inquiry to welcome to magnificence:
You have come around the world to rescue France,

dear cousins. Nothing is too good for you!
Feast now and every visit. Make us your rendezvous.

I checked this with Worths, the senior ones still living:
Didn't you know that? they said. *Don't you know anything?*

Pressure

A man with a neutral face
in the great migration
clutching his shined suitcase
queueing at the Customs station:

Please (yes, you) open your suitcase.
He may not have understood.
Make it snappy. Open it! Come on!
Looking down out of focus did no good.

Tell him to open his suitcase!
The languages behind him were pressure.
He hugged his case in stark reluctance.
Tell him put suitcase on the counter!

Hasps popped, cut cords fell clear
and there was nothing in the suitcase.

Church

i.m. Joseph Brodsky

The wish to be right
has decamped in large numbers
but some come to God
in hopes of being wrong.

High on the end wall hangs
the Gospel, from before he was books.
All judging ends in his fix,
all, including his own.

He rose out of Jewish,
not English evolution
and he said the lamp he held
aloft to all nations was Jewish.

Freedom still eats freedom,
justice eats justice, love —
even love. One retarded man said
church makes me want to be naughty,

but naked in a muddy trench
with many thousands, someone's saying
the true god gives his flesh and blood.
Idols demand yours off you.

Pastoral Sketch

The sex of a stallion at rest
bulges in subtle fine rehearsal,
and his progeny drop in the grass
like little loose bagpipes.
Wet nap and knotty drones, they lie
glazing, and learning air
then they lever upright, wobbling.
Narrow as two dimensions
they nuzzle their mothers' groin
for the yoghurt that makes girth.

The Mare out on the Road

Sliding round the corner on gravel
and there was a mare across the road
and a steep embankment down to the paddock.
The moment was crammed with just two choices.

Sliding fast, with the brakes shoaling gravel.
Five metres down, and would the car capsize?
The moment was crammed with just two choices.
One of two accidents would have to happen.

The poor horse was a beautiful innocent
but her owner never let a grudge go by.
No court case, just family slurs for life.
Sliding fast with the brakes shoaling gravel.

The mare was expanding. Would she run?
leave a gap before or behind to drive through?
No chance. She grew in moist astonishment.
Five metres down, and would the car capsize?

Blood hoof collision would be NOW, without a swerve.
Would the car explode in flames, below? It plunged
aslant, away down. The door groaned up like a hatch.
No court case, just family slurs for life

because the old man didn't believe in accidents,
nor in gestures. The mare trots off
ahead of boots hobbling to find the old man's son.
The poor horse was a beautiful innocent.

The breeder's son on their tractor
was full of apologies and shame, winching
the mouth-full, glass-weeping car back up in secret
because the old man didn't believe in accidents.

The Blueprint

Whatever the great religions offer
it is afterlife their people want:
Heaven, Paradise, higher reincarnations,
together or apart –
for these they will love God, or butter Karma.

Afterlife. Wherever it already exists
people will crawl into ships' framework
or suffocate in truck containers to reach it,
they will conjure it down
on their beaches and their pooled clay streets,
inject it, marry into it.

The secular withholds any obeisance
that is aimed upwards.
It must go declaratively down,
but 'an accident of consciousness
between two eternities of oblivion' –
all of us have done one
of those eternities already, on our ear.

After the second, we require an afterlife
greater and stranger than science gives us now,
life like, then unlike
what mortal life has been.

Blueprint II

Life after death
with all the difficult people
away in a separate felicity.

Norfolk Island

What did they get for England,
the Bounty mutineers?
Tahitian wives, then the discharging
of murder, on an islet walled by sea.

When all the ship-takers were dead
England gave their descendants
this greater island draped like a green
parachute over cliffs and ravines

and pegged with towering furled pines.
All around lay the same blue wall
supplies are still roped and lightered
in over, for the Beauty mountaineers.

They lived in an abandoned gulag.
Trim Georgian houses whose inside
fireplaces astonished the first
of Bounty's neo-Polynesians.

On a Sydney whim, they were driven
out of that guilty settlement:
damn half breeds on Quality Row!
Sick people in their beds on the street —

Go up and live on your allotments!
Now the island is a garden city
in the flown-over ocean,
a godly tan aristocracy

whose children don't seem hostile
and cars buzz them around
their anxiously fostering nation
of big unused fields.

*(Chorus) We got
everything Tahiti got
e-e-xcept the
coconut!*

Birthplace

Right in that house over there
an atom of sharp spilled my sanctum
and I was extruded, brain cuff,
in my terror, in my soap.

My heart wrung its two
already working hands together
but all the other animals
started waking up in my body,

the stale-water frog, the starving-worm;
my nerves' knotwork globe
was filling up with panic writing;
bat wings in my chest caught fire

and I screamed in comic hiccups
all before focus, in the blazing cold –
then I was re-plugged, amid soothe,
on to a new blood that tasted.

Nothing else intense
happened to us, in this village.
My two years' schooltime here
were my last in my own culture,

the one I still get held to
in this place, in working hours.
I love the wry equal humane
and drive in to be held to it.

Lateral Dimensions

Cloudy night –
not enough stars
to make frost

haunted house –
one room the cattle
never would go in

mowing done –
each thing's a ship again
on a wide green harbour

purification –
newspapers soaked in rain
before they are read

an airliner, high –
life falling in from space
to ramify

rodeo bull
he wins every time
then back on the truck

only one car
of your amber necklace
holds a once-living passenger

afternoon plains –
the only hill ahead
is the rising moon

eels'
liquid jostle through the grass
that night of the year

big pelican, begging,
hook through one yellow foot –
and nobody dares

on line
the first motor car
trotting without a horse

joking
in a foreign language
everyone looks down

accused of history
many decide
not to know any

all the colours
of inside a pumpkin –
Mallee forest in rain

Bright Lights on Earth

Luminous electric grist
brushed over the night world:
White Korea, Dark Korea,
tofu detailing all Japan,
Bangkok on a diamond saddle,
snowed-in Java and Bali
circled by shadow isles,
Cairo in its crushed-ice coupe,
dazzling cobwebbed Europe
that we've seen go black.

Now the streetlights don't
switch off for wars. The past
is fuel of glacé continents,
it rims them in stung salt,
Australia in her sparsely starred
flag hammock. Human light
is the building whose walls
are inside. It bleeds the planet
but who could be refused
the glaring milk of Earth?

Panic Attack

The body had a nightmare.
Awake. No need of the movie.

No need of light, to keep hips
and shoulders rotating in bed
on the gimbals of wet eyes.

Pounding heart, chest pains —
should it be the right arm hurting?

The brain was a void
or a blasted-out chamber —
shreds of speech in there,
shatters of lust and prayer.

No one can face their heart
or turn their back on it.

Bowel stumbled to bowl,
emptied, and emptied again
till the gut was a train
crawling in its own tunnel,

slowly dragging the nightmare
down with it, below heart level.
You would not have died

the fear had been too great
but: to miss the ambulance moment —

Relax. In time, your hourglass
will be reversed again.

Sunday on a Country River

After caramel airs of the sugar islands
and their carrying-handle bridges,
we skimmed over salt rainwater
that was reached across by smoke.

Ospreys flew, or sat up castled on sticks
and the shore trees were algal with creeper.
The diked low country on parole from floods
began foreshadowing inland jacaranda.

Below a two-deck bridge and cathedral city
water silver-brown as polarised shades
shook ahead of us, and split
in two behind us like innumerable catch.

We tied up under high oiled gondola-poles.
Fig trees had star-burst the pavements we pubbed on
but the blackboards lunch was scrubbed on
sent us away to cast off for more vista.

Pelicans still luffed aloft
now into air that breathed of cattle, and
front-verandah houses, bland with equality,
perched atop increasing bluffs.

Only a historic Bedouin tent of vast
corrugated iron presided, farther back,
and turning under layered cliffs
we kept causing long wing-skitter takeoffs.

We were nearly to Pages', when our boat
bumped and started cavilling. *It gets hairy from here*,
we said. And there was hair, too,
muddy blonde, growing just underwater.

Ripe in the Arbours of the Nose

Even rippled with sun
the greens of a citrus grove darken
like ocean deepening from shore.
Each tree is full of shade.

A shadowy fast spiral through
and a crow's transfixed an orange
to carry off and mine
its latitudes and longitudes
till they're a parched void scrotum.

alAndalus has an orange grove
planted in rows and shaven above
to form an unwalkable dream lawn
viewed from loggias.
         One level down,
radiance in a fruit-roofed ambulatory.

Mandarin, if I didn't eat you
how could you ever see the sun?
(even I will never see it
except in blue translation).

Shedding its spiral pith helmet
an orange is an irrigation
of rupture and bouquet
rocking the lower head about;

one of the milder borders
of the just endurable
is the squint taste of a lemon,

and it was limes, of dark tooled green
which forgave the barefoot sailors
bringing citrus to new dry lands.

Cumquat, you bitter quip,
let a rat make jam of you
in her beardy house.

Blood orange, children!
raspberry blood in the glass:
look for the five o'clock shadow
on their cheeks.
         Those are full of blood,
and easy: only pick the ones that
relax off in your hand.

Below Hollywood, as everywhere
the trees of each grove appear
as fantastically open
treasure sacks, tied only at the ground.

Industrial Relations

Said the conjuror Could I have afforded
to resign on the spot when you ordered
me to saw the Fat Lady
in half before payday
I would have. I find wage cuts sordid.

From a Tourist Journal

In a precinct of liver stone, high
on its dais, the Taj seems bloc hail.

We came to Agra over honking roads
being built under us, past baby wheat
and undoomed beasts and walking people.
Lorries shouldered white marble loads.

Glamour of ads demeaned street life
in the city; many buildings were
held aloft with liverwurst mortar.
I have not left the Taj Mahal.

Camels were lozenge-clipped like rug pile
and workhorses had kept their stallionhood
even in town, around the Taj wall.
Anglos deny theirs all Bollywood.

On Indian streets, tourists must still
say too much no, and be diminished.
Pedlars speak of it to their lit thumbs.
I have not left the Taj Mahal.

Poor men, though, in Raj-time uniforms:
I'd felt that lure too, and understood.
In Delhi, we craned up at a sky-high
sandstone broom cinched with balustrades.

Schoolkids from Nagaland posed with us
below it, for their brag books, and new cars
streamed left and right to the new world,
but from Agra Fort we'd viewed, through haze,

perfection as a factory making depth,
pearl chimneys of the Taj Mahal.

Definitions

Effete: a pose
of palace cavalry officers
in plum Crimean fig,
spurs and pointed boots,

not at all the stamp
of tight-buttoned guards
executing arm-
                geometry
in the shouting yards,

but sitting his vehicle
listening to tanks change gears
amid oncoming fusiliers
one murmurs the style

that has carried his cohort
to this day, and now will test them:
You have to kill them, Giles,
You can't arrest them.

The Conversations

A full moon always rises at sunset
and a person is taller at night.
Many fear their phobias more than death.
The glass King of France feared he'd shatter.
Chinese eunuchs kept their testes in spirit.

Your brain can bleed from a sneeze-breath.
A full moon always rises at sunset
and a person is taller when prone.
Donald Duck was once banned in Finland
because he didn't wear trousers,

his loins were feather-girt like Daisy's
but no ostrich hides its head in sand.
The cure for scurvy was found
then long lost through medical theory.
The Beginning is a steady white sound.

The full moon rises at sunset
and lemurs and capuchin monkeys
pass a millipede round to get off on
its powerful secretions. Mouthing it
they wriggle in bliss on the ground.

The heart of a groomed horse slows down.
A fact is a small compact faith,
a sense-datum to beasts, a power to man
even if true, even while true –
we read these laws in Isaac Neurone.

One woman had sixty-nine children.
Some lions mate fifty times a day.
Napoleon had a victory addiction.
A full moon always rises at sunset.
Soldiers now can get in the family way.

The Double Diamond

He was the family soldier,
deadly marksman on tropic steeps.

Home, he spurned the drunk heir-splitting
of working for parents, and stayed poor

on share farm after fence-sagging share farm.
Goodbye! yelled the kids to new friends.

Slim sang his songs, and his kind
wife's skin was sensitive to gossip.

Over eighty, he stands in his suit
outside where she, quick-spoken Alice

lies tight-packed in varnished timber.
As the family gather, he tells me

*Late years, I've lived at the hospital.
Now I'll forget the way there.*

As Country Was Slow

for Peter

Our new motorway
is a cross-country fort
and we reinforcements
speed between earthworks
water-sumps and counterscarps,
breaking out on wide glimpses,
flying the overpasses –

Little paper lanterns
march up and down dirt,
wrapped round three chopsticks
plastic shrub-guards grow bushes
to screen the real bush,
to hide the old towns
behind sound-walls and green –

Wildlife crossings underneath
the superglued pavement
are jeep size; beasts must see
nature restart beyond.
The roads are our nature
shining beyond delay,
fretting to race on –

Any check in high speed
can bleed into gravel
and hang pastel wreaths
over roadside crosses.
Have you had your scare yet? –
It made you a driver
not an ever-young name.

We're one Ireland, plus
at least six Great Britains
welded around Mars
and cross-linked by cars –
Benzene, diesel, autobahn:
they're a German creation,
these private world-splicers.

The uncle who farmed our place
was an Arab of his day
growing fuel for the horses
who hauled the roads then.
1914 ended that. Will I
see fuel crops come again?
I'll ride a slow vehicle

before cars are slow
as country was slow.

Midi

Muscles and torsoes of cloud
ascended over the mountains.
The fields looked like high speed
so new-mown was the hay,

then the dark blue Italian lavender
met overhead, a strange maize
deeply planted as mass javelins
in the hoed floor of the land.

Insects in plastic armour stared
from their turrets, and munched
as others machined stiffly over us
and we turned, enchanted
in sweet walling breath
under far-up gables of the lavender.

Observing the Mute Cat

Clean water in the house
but the cat laps up clay water
outside. Drinking the earth.

His pile, being perfect,
ignores the misting rain.

A charcoal Russian
he opens his mouth like other cats
and mimes a greeting mew.

At one bound top-speed across
the lawn and halfway up
the zippy pear tree. Why? Branches?
Stopping puzzles him.

Eloquent of purr
or indignant tail
he politely hates to be picked up.
His human friend never does it.

He finds a voice
in the flyscreen, rattling it,
hanging cruciform on it,
all to be let in
to walk on his man.

He can fish food pellets
out of the dispenser, but waits,
preferring to be served.

A mouse he was playing
on the grass ran in under him.
Disconsolate, at last he wandered
off – and drew and fired
himself in one motion.

He is often above you
and appears where you will go.

He swallows his scent, and
discreet with his few stained birds
he carries them off to read.

Nursing Home

Ne tibi supersis:
don't outlive yourself;
panic, or break a hip
or spit purée at the staff
at the end of gender,
never a happy ender –

yet in the pastel light
of indoors, there is a lady
who has distilled to love
beyond the fall of memory.

She sits holding hands
with an ancient woman
who calls her *brother* and *George*
as bees summarise the garden.

Fame

We were at dinner in Soho
and the couple at the next table
rose to go. The woman paused to say
to me: *I just wanted you to know*
I have got all your cook books
and I swear by them!

    I managed
to answer her: *Ma'am*
they've done you nothing but good!
which was perhaps immodest
of whoever I am.

Cattle-Hoof Hardpan

Trees from modern times don't bear
but the old China pear
still standing in the soil
of 1880 rains fruit.

Phone Canvass

Chatting, after the donation part,
the Blind Society's caller
answered my shy questions:

'. . . and I love it on the street,
all the echo and air pressure,
people in my forehead and
metal stone brick, the buildings
passing in one side of my head . . .

I can hear you smiling.'

Science Fiction

I can travel
faster than light
so can you
the speed of thought
the only trouble
is at destinations
our thought balloons
are coated invisible
no one there sees us
and we can't get out
to be real or present
phone and videophone
are almost worse
we don't see a journey
but stay in our space
just talking and joking
with those we reach
but can never touch
the nothing that can hurt us
how lovely and terrible
and lonely is this.

Brown Suits

Sorting clothes for movie costume,
chocolate suits of hull-market cut,
slim blade ties ending in fringes,
brimmed felt hats, and the sideburned
pork-pie ones that served them. I lived then.

The right grade of suit coat, unbuttoned
can still get you a begrudged free meal
in a café. But seat sweat off sunned vinyl,
ghostly through many dry-cleans
and the first deodorants. I lived then

and worked for the man who abolished
bastards. The prime minister* who
said on air *I'm what you call a bastard.
Illegitimate.* And drove a last stake
through that lousiest distinction.

* *Prime Minister J. G. Gorton (1968–71)*

Southern Hemisphere Garden

This autumn grove, in the half world
that has no fall season, shows a mauve
haze all through its twig-sheaves
and over a rich spangled ground
of Persian leaves.
        Inroads of sun
are razzle gold and textile blond
out to the greens and blady-grass baulks
mown in drought along the pond.
        Thoth
the many ibis lift for the night perches,
the nankeen heron has moved to Japan
but ink-blue waterhens preen long feet
or, flashing undertail
like feathers of the queen protea, run
each other round the brimming rain dam
whose inner sky is black below shine
as if Space were closer, down.
        Back this summer
of the out-of-season Christmas snow
that scotched the bushfires in Victoria
I was out under green leaf-tressed
deciduous, hooking a pole saw
high and snapping down water-stressed
abortive limbs from beneath China
and Europe and America.

Now lichens up
the yeast boughs of those trees are bazaar
trinkets on the belly-dance troupe
at the rural show, who circled sidestepping
to the tappets of a drum.
        'Sacred women's business,'
they laughed after, adjusting coins
over their floured and bake-oil skins,
strolling, antique, unaccusingly bizarre.

The Suspect Corpse

The dead man lay, nibbled, between
dark carriages of a rocky river,

a curled load of himself, in cheap
clothes crusted in dried water.

Noisy awe, nose-crimped, sent us up the
gorge, to jail, in case we were hoaxing.

Following us back down next morning
forensics mentioned his wish bone

but never could pry any
names from between his teeth,

not his own, nor who had lashed
his ankles, or put boulders in his clothes.

After three months, he could only
generalise, and had started smiling.

Eucalypts in Exile

They've had so many jobs:
boiling African porridge. Being printed on.
Sopping up malaria. Flying in Paris uprisings.
Supporting a stork's nest in Spain.

Their suits are neater abroad,
of denser drape, un-nibbled:
they've left their parasites at home.

They flower out of bullets
and, without any taproot,
draw water from way deep.
Blown down in high winds
they reveal the black sun of that trick.

Standing around among shed limbs
and loose craquelure of bark
is home-country stuff
but fire is ingrained.
They explode the mansions of Malibu
because to be eucalypts
they have to shower sometimes in Hell.

Their humans, meeting them abroad,
often grab and sniff their hands.

Loveable singly or unmarshalled
they are merciless in a gang.

Cherries from Young

Cherries from Young
that pretty town,
white cherries and black,
sun-windows on them.

Cherries from Young
the tastiest ever
grow in drought time
on farms above there.

One lip-teased drupe
or whole sweet gallop
poured out of cardboard
in whatever year,

cherries from Young.
All the roads back
go down into Young
that early town.

Croc

This police car with a checkered seam
of blue and white teeth along its side
lies in cover like a long-jawed
flat dog beside the traffic stream.

High-speed Bird

At full tilt, air gleamed –
and a window-struck kingfisher,
snatched up, lay on my palm
still beating faintly.

Slowly, a tincture
of whatever consciousness is
infused its tremor, and
ram beak wide as scissors

all hurt loganberry inside,
it crept over my knuckle
and took my outstretched finger
in its wire foot-rings.

Cobalt wings, shutting on beige
body. Gold under-eye whiskers,
beak closing in recovery
it faced outward from me.

For maybe twenty minutes
we sat together, one on one,
as if staring back or
forward into prehistory.

The Cowladder Stanzas

Not from a weather direction
black cockatoos come crying over
unflapping as Blériot monoplanes
to crash in pine tops for the cones.

Young dogs, neighbours' dogs
across the creek, bark, chained
off the cows, choked off play, bark
untiring as a nightsick baby, yap
milking times to dark, plead,
ute-dancing dope-eye dogs.

Red-hot pokers up and out
of their tussock. Kniphofia flowers
overlapping many scarlet jubes
form rockets on a stick.
Ignition's mimed by yellow petticoats.

Like all its kind
Python has a hare lip
through which it aims its tongue
at eye-bursting Hare.

Thinking up names
for a lofty farm: High Wallet,
Cow Terraces, Fogsheep,
Rainside, Helmet Brush,
Tipcamber, Dingo Leap.

My boyhood farm cousin spoke
French, and I understood fluently
but not in this world.
It happened just one time
in my early urban sleep.

I know — as they may prefer —
little of the beekeeper family
who've lived for years inside
tall kindling of their forest
in old car bodies, sheds
and the rotted like sailcloth
of their first shore day.

And the blue wonga pigeon
walks under garden trees
and pumpkins lean like wheels
out of their nurturing trash.

We climbed the Kokoda Track.
Goura pigeon, rain, kau kau.
Dad said after the war
they wanted soldier settlement
blocks in New Guinea. This was struck
down by a minister named Hasluck.
Paul Hasluck. Dad's grateful now:
it would have been bloody Mau Mau.

The Farm Terraces

Beautiful merciless work
around the slopes of earth
terraces cut by curt hoe
at the orders of hunger
or a pointing lord.
Levels eyed up to rhyme
copied from grazing animals
round the steeps of earth,
balconies filtering water
down stage to stage of drop.
Wind-stirred colours of crop
swell between walked bunds
miles of grass-rimmed contour
harvests down from the top
by hands long in the earth.
Baskets of rich made soil
boosted up poor by the poor,
ladder by freestone prop
stanzas of chant-long lines
by backwrenching slog, before
money, gave food and drunk

but rip now like slatted sails
(some always did damn do)
down the abrupts of earth.

Visiting Geneva

I came to Geneva
by the bullet train,
up from church kero lamps –
it must have been the bullet train.

I rolled in on a Sunday
to that jewelled circling city
and everything was closed
in the old-fashioned way.

In the city of Palais
and moored Secretariat
I arrived in spring when
the Ferraris come out.

Geneva, refuge of the Huguenots,
Courtauld, Pierrepoint, Haszard,
Boers Joubert and Marais,
Brunel's young Isambard

and John Calvin, unforgiver
in your Taliban hat,
you pervade bare St Peter's
in la France protestante,

Calvin, padlock of the sabbath,
your followers now protect you:
predestination wasn't yours, they claim,
nor were the Elect you,

but: when you were God
sermons went on all day
without numen or presence.
Children were denied play.

I had fun with your moral snobbery
but your great work's your recruits,
your Winners and Losers. You
turned mankind into suits –

and many denims, messer John.

The Bronze Bull

Went down to Wall Street
and the Bull it was gone
the mighty bronze one
squat lord of Wall Street.
A year and a half
before the subprime
not even a calf
wore bronze on that small street,

some skyscrapers may have.
Squared flow-lines, tight-packed,
are the charging Bull's style.
In battle with his Squaremacht
the dumpy brown Allies
were brave in round turrets
or ice-shaggy as the Bear
but they took home Bull's power.

Haven't been back
among Wall Street diviners
where the long green's assigned its
hourly valuations.

Don't know if the hoof-scraping
humpmaster of freedom
is back in place there
or off fighting Baby Bear.

Port Jackson Greaseproof Rose

Which spawned more civilisations,
yellow grass or green?

Who made poverty legal?
Who made poverty at all?

Eating a cold pork sandwich
out of greaseproof paper
as I cross to Circular Quay
where the world-ships landed poverty
on the last human continent
where it had not been known.

Linked men straddling their chains
being laughed at by naked people.

This belongs to my midlife:
out of my then suburban city
rise towers of two main kinds,
new glass ones keyed high to catch money
and brown steeples to forgive the poor

who made poverty illegal
and were sentenced here for it.

And the first jumbo jets descend
like mates whose names you won't recall,
going down behind the city.

The Springfields

Lead drips out of
a burning farm rail.
Their Civil War.

Rugby Wheels

i.m. Matt Laffan 1970–2009

Four villages in Ireland
knew never to mix their blood
but such lore gets lost
in the emigrations.
Matt Laffan's parents learned it
in their marriage of genes

they could never share again.
They raised Matt through captaincies
and law degrees. And he exalted them
with his verve and clarities,
sat on a rugby tribunal,
drank beers a third his height

and rode a powered wheelchair
akimbo as in a chariot
with tie-clip, combed red hair,
causes to plead. Beloved in Sydney
he created a travel website
for the lame, and grinned among them

Doors will often open.
Beware a step or two
down or up when they do,
and he told self-doubters
You'll always be taller than me!
as he flew his electoral box-kite.

Popular with women, and yet
vision of him in their company
often shows a precipice near
or a balcony-lit corridor.
I would have lacked his
heroism in being a hero.

A Frequent Flyer Proposes a Name

Sexburga Drive is a steep mud lane
but Sexburga, she was Queen of Kent
fourteen centuries ago.
She tried to rule as well as reign
but her tough spear-thanes grated No!
she's but a wife-man, a loaf-kneader:
we will not obey a bodice-feeder.
No precedent, said Witan. Quite unkent
so on Sheppey isle she built a convent.

But now, in an era more Amazon,
the notion has come to the jarl of London,
white-polled Boris, to move Heathrow
east to the marshy Thames outflow
so jetliners may leave their keening cry
out over the Channel and grim North Sea –
and Celtic queens have ruled: Boudicca, Bess,
but your Saxon ones still await redress
so savour this name: London Sexburga Airport.

Hesiod on Bushfire

Poxes of the Sun or of the mind
bring the force-ten firestorms.
After come same-surname funerals,
junked theory, praise of mateship.

Love the gum forest, camp out in it
but death hosts your living in it, brother.
You need buried space
and cellars have a convict foetor:

only pubs kept them. Houses shook them off
wherever Diggers moved to.
Only opal desert digs homes by dozer,
the cool Hobbit answer.

Cellars, or bunkers, mustn't sit square
under the fuel your blazing house will be,
but nearby, roofed refractory,
tight against igniting air–miles.

Power should come underground
from Fortress Suburbia, and your treasures
stay back there, where few now
grow up in the fear of grass.

Never build on a summit or a gully top:
fire's an uphill racer deliriously welcomed
by growth it cures of growth.
Shun a ridgeline, window puncher at a thousand degrees.

Sex is Fire, in the ancient Law.
Investment is Fire. Grazing beasts are cool Fire
backburning paddocks to the door.
Ideology is Fire.

The British Isles and giant fig trees are Water.
Horse-penis helicopters are watery TV
but unblocked roads and straight volunteers
are lifesaving spume spray.

Water and Fire chase each other in jet
planes. May you never flee through them
at a generation's end, as when
the Great Depression died, or Marvellous Melbourne.

The Blame

for Clare

Archie was a gun to shoot at biplanes
and an uncle I missed meeting, a dancing whiz
till we lost the footwork that was his.

His elder brother was a timbercutter
who scorned to fell a rotting tree
so their father wheedled hapless Archie

who dropped it crooked, into his brain.
All would rather he had left children
on earth than the mighty grief that followed.

His mother had seen the head-splash happen
five hours before it did, and rode
searching the bush to find the men.

She saw because she knew her world.
Later she would ask her husband
Did you even take your own axe, Allan?

Face and bequests were the family-labour system
so the expert brother got his owed block
with a weatherproof dairy and bung clock.

Everything else let the wind through.
Neither he nor his father believed in accident.
Punishment was happening. He was charged rent

to preclude any loans for farm improvement.
Some had always scorned his town wife's dignity
and his brother's name cried out in dreams.

He, the blamed son, loved all his mother gave him,
the gold watch, touring car, touch of fey;
the latter two failed on his wife's death day

but the car was kept till it fell apart.
Archie's name was shunned, its luck was bad,
but all his survivors got the farm we'd had.

Now nearly everyone who knew an Archie
has gone to join him in memory.
Freed of blood, the name starts to return.

Daylight Cloth

September morning. White is salient.
The unfocussed wet hover of dawn
has cleared the treetops. In high bush
the ski season packs up, tent by tent,

and the Cherokee rose, its new seams
hitched up rather than pruned,
overlaps its live willow easel,
a daylight cloth pelted in white creams.

Minute blossoms of fruit
emerge from lichen's brown wheeze
that has gathered in their trees.
Burnt-off paddocks have gone out

and the sky is bluer for it.
Beyond the sea coast, rebirthed
four-wheel drives tilt, below,
on the tail ends of big seas.

The Mirrorball

Half a day's drive from Melbourne
until we reach the first town
that's not bypassed by expressway.
Holbrook, once Germantown,
Holbrook of the submarines,
conning tower and periscopes
rising out of sheep land.

It recalls the country towns
up the roads of 1940
each with its trees and Soldier,
its live and dead shop windows
and a story like Les Boyce
we heard about up home,
Taree's Lord Mayor of London.

But now song and story are pixels
of a mirrorball that spins celebrities
in patter and tiny music
so when the bus driver restarts
his vast tremolo of glances
half his earplugged sitters wear
the look of deserted towns.

Infinite Anthology

Gross motor – co-ordination as a whistle subject
audiation – daydreaming in tunes
papped – snapped by paparazzi
whipping side – right-hand side of a convict or sheep
hepcat, hip (from Wolof *hipi-kat,* one who knows the score) –
    spirit in which modernist art goes slumming
instant – (Australian) Nescafé
ranga – redhead

Creators of single words or phrases are by far the largest class of poets. Many ignore all other poetry.

Jail tats — totemic underskin writing done because illegal
lundy — a turned Ulster
rebuttal tapes — counter-propaganda filmed by warplanes
free traders — (19th and early 20th cent.) split bloomers worn
    under voluminous skirts
daylight — second placegetter when winner is very superior to
    field
window licker — a voyeur
fibro — resident of a poorer suburb

Single-word poets hope to be published and credited in the Great Book of Anon, the dictionary. The cleverest make their names serve this purpose: Maxim, Maxim's, Churchillian.

Irishtown — a Soweto of old-time Catholic labour
'bunny boiler — one who kills her offspring
dandruff acting — the stiffest kind of Thespian art
blackout — Aboriginal party or picnic, whites not invited
butternut — homespun cloth dyed with hickory juice
shart — a non-dry fart
Baptist Boilermaker — coffee and soda (an imagined Puritan
    cocktail)

Single-word poets recycle words in advance of need, or leave them exposed to the weather of real difference.

Wedge — cloth bunched in the groin; may cause camel toe (q.v.)
wedge — to force the pace or direction
bushed — lost (Australian)
bushed — tired (American)
bushed — suffering camp fever (Canadian)
limo — limousin cattle
proud — castrated but still interested

Individual words, with their trains of definition loosening around them, allow us to visit the oracular and sense its renewing dance.

Drummy – echoing, hollow-sounding (mining term)
rosebud – American Civil War wound
Shabbos goy – Gentile who does small jobs for Orthodox Jews
    on Sabbath or other holy days
choke – to strap loose freight tightly together for transport
off book – (theatre) having one's lines down pat
bugle driver – attachment on a drill to intensify its power in
    sinking screws
tipping elbow – (Aboriginal) sneaking glances at one's watch

Manuscript Roundel

What did you see in the walnut?
Horses red-harnessed criss cross
and a soldier wearing the credits
of his movie like medal ribbons.
An egg in there building a buttery
held itself aloft in its hands –
red straps then pulled the nut shut.

Natal Grass

Plain as wicker most of the year
along October this tousled grass
wakes up on road verges in a smoke
of sago bloom, of ginger knots
tied in a shapeless woolly plasma

but get this web across the sun
and it ignites cut-glass rosé
goblets and pitchers. In God's name
liquid opal from a parallel shore,
the dazzle of dew any time of day.

The Black Beaches

Yellow rimming the ocean
is mountains washing back
but lagoons in cleared land often
show beaches of velvet black

peat of grass and great trees
that were wood-fired towers
then mines of stary coals
fuming deep in dragon-holes.

This morning's frost dunes
afloat on knee-sprung pasture
were gone in a sugar lick
leaving strawed moisture

but that was early
and a change took back the sun
hiding it in regrowth forest.
Coal formed all afternoon.

Inspecting the Rivermouth

Drove up to Hahndorf:
boiled lamb hock, great scoff!
Lamplit rain incessant.

Next morning to the Murray mouth,
reed-wrapped bottlings of view
grigio and verdelho.

Saw careers from the climbing bridge,
the steel houses it threw
all over Hindmarsh Island,

the barrages de richesse,
film culture, horseradish farms,
steamboats kneading heron-blue

lake, the river full again.
Upstream, the iron cattle bridges.
So. Then a thousand miles

home across green lawn.

High Rise

Fawn high rise of Beijing
with wristwatch-shaped
air conditioners on each window

and burglar bars to the tenth
level in each new city,
white-belted cylinders of dwelling

around every Hong Kong bay –
Latest theory is, the billions
will slow their overbreeding

only when consuming in the sky.
Balconious kung fu of Shanghai.
A nineteenth-floor lover

heroic among consumer goods
slips off the heights of desire
down the going-home high wire –

above all the only children.

Nuclear Family Bees

Little native-bee hives
clotted all up the trunk
of a big tree by the river.

Not pumped from a common womb
this world of honey-flies
is a vertical black suburb

of glued-on prism cells.
Hunters stopping by
would toe-walk up,

scab off single wax houses
and suck them out, as each
smallholder couple hovered

remonstrating in the air
with their life to rebuild,
new eggs, new sugarbag,

gold skinfuls of water.

When Two Per Cent Were Students

Gorgeous expansion of life
all day at the university –
then home to be late for tea,
an impractical, unwanted boarder.

When rush hours were so tough
a heart attack might get stepped over
you looked up from the long footpaths
to partings in the houses' iron hair.

Hosts of depression and wartime
hated their failure, which was you.
Widows with no facelift of joy
spat their irons. Shamed by bookishness

you puzzled their downcast sons
who thought you might be a poofter,
and you'd hitch home to run wild
again where cows made vaccines

and ancient cows discovered aspirin,
up home, where your father and you
still wore pink from the housework
you taught each other years before,

and those were the years when farm wives
drove to the coast with milk hands
to gut fish, because government no longer
trusted poor voters on poor lands.

I Wrote a Little Haiku

I wrote a little haiku
titled *The Springfields*:

Lead drips out of
a burning farm rail.
Their Civil War.

Critics didn't like it,
said it was obscure –

The title was the rifle
both American sides bore,
lead was its heavy bullet
the Minié, which tore

often wet with blood and sera
into the farmyard timbers
and forests of that era,
wood that, burnt even now,

might still re-melt and pour
out runs of silvery ichor
the size of wasted semen
it had annulled before.

West Coast Township

Cervantes. This one-strum pueblo
seen beyond acorn banksia
along a Benedictine surf –
never the Oz end of a cable, though.

How Spanish was the Indian Ocean?

Well, not. Except for basque Sebastian
de Elcano, centuries off Perth:
*Of mankind, only we in my ship shall
have made a full circuit of Earth . . .*

even as scurvy kept their ebb low.

Money and the Flying Horses

Intriguing, the oaten seethe
of thoroughbred horses in single stalls
across a twilit cabin.

Intimate, under the engines' gale,
a stamped hoof, a loose-lip sigh,
like dawn sounds at track work.

Pilots wearing the bat wings
of intercontinental night cargo
come out singly, to chat with or warn

the company vet at his manifests:
four to Dubai, ten from Shannon,
Singapore, sixteen, sweating their nap.

They breed in person, by our laws:
halter-snibbed horses radiating over the world.
Under half-human names, they run in person.

We dress for them, in turn. Our officer class
fought both of its world wars in riding tog:
Luftwaffe and Wehrmacht in haunched jodhpur pants.

Stumbling turbulence, and the animals
skid, swivelling their large eyes
but iron-fisted rear-outs calmed by revolver shot

are a rarity now, six miles above
the eventing cravat, the desert hawking dunes.
Handlers move among the unroofed stalls.

They're settling down now, Hank:
easy to tell, with stallions;
they must be the nudest creatures alive –

Tomorrow, having flown from money to money
this consignment will be trucked and rested
then, on cobble, new hands will assume the familiar

cripple-kneed buttock-up seat
of eighteenth century grooms
still used by jockeys.

Sun Taiko

Across the river
outside towns
farm machinery for sale
in wire compounds

Pumpkin to all of it
are rainwater tanks
plastic, mostly round
edge on, ribby flanks
a few Roman IIIs

all in cool Kiwi tones
sage, battleship, dun
two thousand litres, ten
each with a rimmed
O hole for sound

Child Logic

The smallest girl
in the wild kid's gang
submitted her finger
to his tomahawk idea –

It hurt bad, dropping off.
He knew he'd gone too far
and ran, herding the others.
Later on, he'd maim her brother.

She stayed in the bush
till sundown, wrote
in blood on the logs, and
gripped her gapped hand, afraid

what her family would say
to waste of a finger.
Carelessness. Mad kids.
She had done wrong some way.

Powder of Light

Hunched in the farm ute
tarpaulin against wind
the moon chasing treetops
as it yellows into night
us, going to the pictures
by the State forest way
my mate's brother driving

we are at the age
that has since slipped
down toward toddlers
for whom adults and dreams
mostly have no names yet.
What wagged on screen then
made from powder of light

were people in music
who did and said dressy
stuff in English or American
kissed slow with faces crossed
flicked small-to-big
in an instant, then
were back in Australia

we believed it was Australia —
then our driver who never
attended films would surface
from courting and collect us
there way before TV.

And people, some holding
phones like face cards, still ask

good movie? Who was in it?
I smile and say *Actors*
but rarely now add
hired out of the air.

Index of Titles

Index of First Lines